RHINESTONES!

A COLLECTOR'S HANDBOOK & PRICE GUIDE

Nancy N. Schiffer

77 Lower Valley Road, Atglen, PA 19310

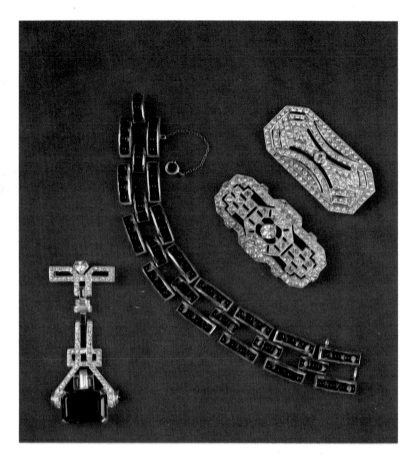

Above photo:
Elegant jewelry set with rhinestones of
faceted and cabochon shapes. These
designs from the 1930s are probably
French. Cobra and Bellamy

Title page photo:
Jeweled "Maltese Cross" necklace and
matching earclips made c. 1971 by R.F.
Clark for Wm. de Lillo USA. With German
crystal faceted stones in silver plated metal.
Wm. de Lillo Archive

Opposite:
At left, clear rhinestone cuff bracelet by
Nina Ricci, circa 1970. At right top, a
German link bracelet of pink, black and
clear rhinestones mounted in silver, circa
1930. Center, an American green paste
link bracelet circa 1930. Bottom, an all-
clear German link bracelet set in silver, c.
1930. Cobra and Bellamy

Copyright © 1993 by Schiffer Publishing, Ltd.
Library of Congress Catalog Number:
  92-63100.

Printed in the United States of America.
ISBN: 0-88740-457-X

Published by Schiffer Publishing, Ltd.
77 Lower Valley Road
Atglen, PA 19310
Please write for a free catalog.
This book may be purchased from the publisher.
Please include $2.95 postage.
Try your bookstore first.

We are interested in hearing from authors
with book ideas on related subjects.

Contents

Acknowledgements 4
1. Rhinestone History 5
2. Diverse shapes of rhinestones
    Faceted stones 21
    Cabochons 27
    Pendants and drops 33
    Scalloped stones 39
    Unique designs 43
    Special effects 47
    Beads 55
3. Rhinestones in a spectrum of colors
    Clear—diamond, crystal, white topaz 61
    Blue—sapphire, turquoise, aquamarine, lapis lazuli 77
    Green—jade, emerald 89
    Red—ruby, garnet, carnelian 97
    Pink—rose quartz, coral 107
    Purple—amethyst 113
    White—ivory, moonstone, opal 117
    Grey—Smoky topaz, diamond 121
    Black—jet, onyx 125
    Yellow and Brown—amber, topaz, citrine 129
    Pearl 137
4. Combined colors and stones 145
    References 157
    Price Guide 158
    Index 160

Acknowledgements

The assistance of many people in preparing this book has given me new friends among kindred spirits and a broader understanding of the costume industry at large. Each person has taught me from their experience, and guided my questions to be more precise. In each case, we shared a concern and found some answers.

My thanks are specifically offered to Terry Schreiner Albert, of Schreiner jewelry, and Otto Hoffer of E.H. Ashley & Co. in Providence, R.I. who made their collections and their knowledge available to me.

Jewelry designers William de Lillo and Robert Clark of William de Lillo USA provided their personal knowledge of the jewelry industry, in the 1960's especially, and furnished beautifully documented examples from their archives.

Jewelry collectors Beebe Hopper, Adeline Trievel and Peggy Osborne opened their jewelry boxes to share their treasures with the readers.

Jewelry dealers Elsa Rothstein Zukin and Joan Rothstein Toborowsky of E & J Rothstein Antiques, Pat Funt, Lawrence Feldman of Fior, Cobra and Bellamy, Bel Arte, and Francis Cronin of Franny's all shared their personal and business collections for the reader's enjoyment. My gratitude is extended to each of you.

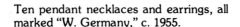

Ten pendant necklaces and earrings, all marked "W. Germany," c. 1955.

1. Rhinestone History

Natural gemstones are so glamorous that the compulsion to emulate them has grown among all people who occupy themselves with decorating the human body. And "emulate" is the most you can hope for since natural gems are unique. Substitutes for gemstones have a history, based in Europe, which is closely tied to the development of the glass industry. Ancient and medieval glassmakers were largely concerned with creating imitation gemstones. Venetian glass shops in the fourteenth century exported handmade gemstones to all parts of Europe and supported an enormous world trade. By the 16th century, faceting was introduced to bring out the reflective properties of diamonds and colored gems. But not until the late nineteenth century were glass stones cut by machine, which enabled the production of a sufficient quantity of stones to make it a viable business.

Machine-made stones have come to be known as "rhinestones," a word with origins in Austrian history. In the early decades of the twentieth century, a few tourist shops along the banks of the Rhine river sold jewelry with stones called "Rheinkiesel." These were water-clear stones which were cut like diamonds, and had red, green and blue blotches inside. They were made from glass molded and cut in Bohemia, and the red, green, and blue patches had been ingeniously fused into the clear glass during the molding process. "Rheinkiesel," literally translated, means "Rhine pebbles." Whether the tourists believed that the "stones" had been fished out of the river, or simply bought them for their attractive appearance as souvenirs to take home

Matching set marked "Austria."

Two sets of pins and earrings marked
"West Germany," with filigree metal work
and iridescent stones.

from their trip cannot be known. At some point a businessman, probably an American importer, gave the small imitation diamonds from Austria the name "Rhinestones," and to this day the public recognizes them under that name. [Otto Hoffer, "Imitation Gemstones," p. 54 and interview August 6, 1992.]

The Developing Glass Industry in Europe

The European glass industry evolved out of a tradition which probably started in Egypt 5000 years ago. Glass-making was known in Carthage, Phoenicia and Etruria several centuries before Christ. When the Romans occupied Northern Italy, they melted glass and made panes, pots, beads and artificial gemstones. The concept is not new.

Through trade, Roman glass objects were carried throughout Gaul and Germania. Early glass manufacturing in German monasteries, in the Rhineland especially, can be traced to the Roman era. At the same time, Syria and parts of the Orient had glass factories based on the Egyptian methods. By medieval times, glassware came into Europe from the Orient. When the Roman Empire collapsed and Germanic tribes occupied the Italian peninsula, glass-making died out there. But it survived in the Eastern Roman Empire of Byzantium and from there glass craftsmen migrated to Persia and to Italy. In the thirteenth century, the island of Murano at Venice became the center for glass-makers who closely guarded their secret formulas against foreign competition.

Two pins: tulip shape marked "Austria,"
and chrysanthemum shape with filigree
metal petals marked "Made in Austria."

In 1295, Marco Polo proved that Venetian glass beads and stones of various colors could be sold to the Orient. Later, explorers such as Columbus and Cortez used Venetian glass beads in trade with natives of the New World and Africa. Soon glass trade goods circled the globe.

Bohemia

Glass-makers from Saxony and Silesia were first lured into Bohemia in the fourteenth century, as over the next two hundred years the vast forest was penetrated by roads linking remote monasteries. To this day Bohemian garnets and other natural transparent materials are cut near the town of Turnau. The town of Gablonz is first mentioned as a village in 1350. By the sixteenth century, glass-making was organized by the landed gentry of the area who saw its business potential. The natural materials were abundant in quartz, potash and wood for fuel.

As the glass industry and trade routes became established, the craftsmen became very specialized. Fashions for glass stones became important in the Austrian Empire, France and Britain and the Bohemian workers met the demand with astonishing hand-crafted glass objects. Jewelry, beads, and buttons were created for each market. In the second half of the nineteenth century, the industry around Gablonz included villages within a thirty-mile radius and employed thousands of people. Their products included chandelier parts, buttons and hollowware, but the heart of the industry was the stones and beads used for costume jewelry and exported to all continents. The United

Very fine, hand set bracelet of delicate filigree metalwork and colored stones from Germany or Austria, c.1930.

States was the largest customer.

There was an active jewelry industry around Gablonz, too, which used the locally made glass stones and beads. The glass stones were cut laboriously and slowly by hand, with eight facets on the front of the stone, eight facets on the back, and a flat table. They were expensive, irregular and available only in small quantities. Experimentation in machine-cutting produced stones that did not have the thick, clumsy edges to which jewelry setters were accustomed. Therefore, the delicate edges were chipped during the setting process.

D. Swarovski & Co.: Bohemia and Austria

In 1891, a young mechanical genius named Daniel Swarovski from the Gablonz area of Bohemia built a machine to cut large quantities of glass stones with precise uniformity and high polish. Swarovski had worked since 1883 in his small, family-owned business making riveted glass jewelry. This business was one of many in the area that had grown to supply Western markets, particularly Paris, through exporters in Gablonz. Daniel continued to experiment with his new ideas for machinery to cut glass very thin, "and soon the manufacture of thin-cut glass articles appeared in the place of riveted glass jewelry." [Swarovski, p. 2] He joined his future father-in-law to found the firm Eduard Weis and Company which "made primarily hat-pins and brooches . . . and delivered our products direct to Paris without the intermediary of a Gablonz exporter. This business grew livelier and livelier."[Swarovski, p.2]

Eduard Weis and Company moved to a small factory in 1886, but in 1888, the business slumped and closed due to changes in fashions. Daniel took a job with an exporter in Gablonz, but continued to experiment. "A workshop of my own was made available to me and my first experiments involved the manufacture of metal beads which were very much in demand at the time. The experiments actually turned out well, but before the practical manufacture of this article was found, the demand had diminished. I invented a new type of button loop which the firm of Richter manufactured and which was passed on to our button suppliers. Then I became involved for several months with the manufacture of different colored, primarily black, cut glass beads which were used in chess ornamentation. These beads were made out of small, six-sided glass rods [of] about 2 to 3mm diameter and 1mm holes."[Swarovski, p.3] Ten to 120 of these uniform beads were made at the same time using Swarovski's improved method.

In 1891, Daniel Swarovski left the exporter in Gablonz to continue his experiments with the Weis firm at Johannensthal, not far away. Here, he concerned himself "primarily with the manufacture of cut punches, which were used for the so-called diamond-cut, a substitute for stones set in metal. At the same time my brother Emil pointed out to me that the need for the small crystal stones was very great and that we could also get orders for these. These stones were from one to ten centimeters in diameter and cut in the manner of diamonds. At that time they were made primarily in the Czech area of Bohemia by small farmers beside their farm work. Even school children had to help with this work." [Swarovski, p. 3]..."The finished stones were delivered primarily to the Gablonz exporters who exported primarily to Paris and to England. North America, which certainly could have used more stones, could only import very small quantities because of the high duty [imposed to protect a small glass-producing business in New England]. [Otto Hoffer interview.] In foreign countries, but also in Gablonz, there were more and more jewelry manufacturing firms which made the stones into pleasing jewelry which was greatly in demand. It is thus understandable that the need for the jewelry stones became ever greater and that the hitherto existing manufacturers who produced stones as a sideline to their actual work could not produce the stones in the desired quantities. . . exporters were interested in finding suppliers who were in a position to deliver large quantities continuously. I began to be interested in this business and concerned myself with finding suitable production methods in order to enter in at the relatively low prices which were being paid for these articles. It was obvious to me that the hitherto existing production would not be suitable for us as we, the Sudeten Germans, in contrast to our Czech competition, had a much higher living standard and worked with

"Dimensional Geometric" jeweled brooch, earclips and hinged cuff bracelet made with Swarovski pink crystal cabochon ribbon, from the Disco collection, c. 1970-71, designed by R. F. Clark for Wm. de Lillo USA. Wm. de Lillo Archive

well-paid people. So I constructed and built a very simple device [to cut stones many at a time]. . .The stones cut this way were more regular and significantly nicer than those made before. Thus, the first cutting apparatus was invented, and in 1892. . .I registered a patent in my name in Prague."[Swarovski, p.4]

Daniel Swarovski's cutting machine revolutionized the jewelry business. The uniformly cut stones produced in any quantity that they desired gave jewelry manufacturers the inspiration to create entirely new designs. From that time on, cut glass stones were mounted in silver- and gold-plated settings. The increase in the demand for cut glass stones enabled the small town of Gablonz to grow significantly. The mechanized businesses as well as independent hand-cutters expanded to meet the increased demand.

Working with his extended family and some outside financial support, Daniel Swarovski continued to develop more and better water-driven machinery. Expansion of their operation soon proved necessary. To avoid obvious copying of technologies by their competition, and to take advantage of a far greater source of water power in the Bavarian Alp mountains, Swarovski and his firm chose to relocate to Wattens, Austria, near Innsbruck, in 1895.

Continuing to use raw glass materials from Gablonz, the new operation specialized in cutting the stones into finished fancy shapes for jewelry. In the first year at Wattens, about two hundred packets, containing about 1200 pieces each, of chatons (small round cut stones) were produced for sale to the dealers in Paris who sent them to clients in America, England and Germany. Improvements in the machinery were constantly necessary, and the staff, while growing, needed to be trained for each operation. Success brought new demands, but the firm developed new ways of handling them.

By 1900, the company, which numbered about one hundred employees, "could make stones in any size down to under 1mm with ease and greatest precision. When one looked at a packet of such stones, one could really think that one was looking at real diamonds." [Swarovski, p.8] These fine stones have since become associated with the German Tyrol and are popularly called "rhinestones."

Around 1907, the "main glass supplier in Gablonz, who made by far the best composition glass, suddenly got it into his head to cut stones himself and give [the Watterns firm] competition." [Swarovski, p. 15]... "So it seemed to us an act of self-preservation in answer to this action to make ourselves independent through setting up a glass factory of our own. So we ventured with our own vigor and without specialists, to build a glass factory in Wattens."[Swarovski, p.16] Experimentation proceeded in 1908 and continued for three years in relative secrecy which culminated in the building of a separate glass laboratory away from the cutting operation, and the establishment of a new firm, D.

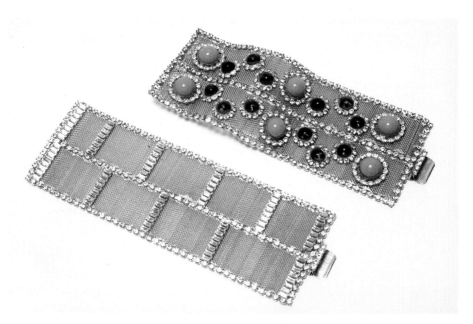

Two wide jeweled "Mesh" cuff bracelets set with Swarovski crystal faux diamond baguette and round stones, c. 1968, designed by R. F. Clark for Wm. de Lillo USA. Wm. de Lillo Archive

Jeweled "Moon" brooch and matching drop earrings with faceted stones from Swarovski, and German glass cabochon aquamarine designe c. 1969 by R.F. Clark for Wm. de Lillo USA. Wm. de Lillo Archive

Swarovski and Company. The town of Wattens developed from a tiny mountain village in 1895 into an industrial town, due largely to the Swarovski and other new firms.

The First World War changed life in Europe forever. No longer would a ruling class lead the population, but through their own talents, individuals would be developed into new leaders. When all existing grinding materials were needed by the Austrian government for the war effort, the Swarovski group resorted to making their own, since delivery from their usual sources was not dependable. Experimentation took place in 1918 until a suitable combination of materials and techniques provided satisfactory results. By 1922, orders for jewelry stores started coming in again, as well as orders for finished grinding stones for sale to other companies in other countries. The Swarovski company thus grew again. Experimentation continued as refinements were deemed necessary. In 1931, the company introduced rhinestone banding, a woven product made with textile threads, synthetic resin, and their jewelry stones, to take up the slack from the decline in the market for gemstone-covered combs. The trend for women to have short-cut, easy-to-manage hair styles reversed the fashion for complex hairdos, and as the fashion changed, so did the market for combs.

The growth of D. Swarovski and Company both led and reflected the growth of the rhinestone industry in Bohemia, Austria and Bavaria at the turn of the twentieth century. By the first decade of the new century, machine-cut stones in the small rhinestone sizes were firmly established on the market and stonesetters had learned to adapt their techniques to the new, refined rhinestones. In the 1920's, the Swarovski firm began producing larger stones and stones in different shapes. The immediate popularity of the new stones was felt in the jewelry market. Designers began executing daring designs to utilize the unusual shapes and textures of glass stones. "Around 1927, a tremendous fashion for sparkling faceted stones developed in the United States lasting for several years, and this encouraged further diversification of the line of Swarovski products."[Hoffer, "Imitation Rhinestones," p.43]

A number of factories were in existence or were founded around Gablonz between 1900 and 1929 to cut glass stones mechanically. Perhaps the leading firm was that of Josef Riedel. From that time to the present, almost all imitations of diamonds and other faceted precious stones have been produced with mechanical devices. Many new designs for jewelry were made in the 1930's utilizing colored rhinestones with increasing frequency. Colored enamels were sometimes combined with the stones to produce naturalistic animal and floral designs. In the 1940's, when jewelry of precious metal and gemstones was too much of a luxury for most consumers, costume

Three pair of earrings and two brooches,
all marked "Austria."

Jewelry designed by Mitchell Maer for Christian Dior. Necklace with grey pearls c. 1952. Necklace and bracelet with turquoise stones c. 1953. Fior

jewelry took a strong position in the shops. Patriotic colors could be worked into the jewelry with colored glass stones easily—as the many remaining pieces of this jewelry can testify.

Austria and Neugablonz

The Second World War disrupted the glass industry in Bohemia as it did all others. The Bohemian territory had been settled by both Czech and Sudeten German people who each felt strong nationalistic ties to the land. In 1945, when Czechoslovakia became free from Nazi domination, the government expelled the minority Sudeten German population. While the export business in Gablonz continued much in the same way it had for a few years, by 1948 the government controls had tightened and exports practically ceased to the United States. [Hoffer, p.32]

a butterfly pin

with shimmering wings
... gold colored stones
5.50*
matching ear clips 4.00*

a sparkling "gold" bag

crushed leather with shining gold tone finish 14.00*
plus Fed. tax

and her favorite seamless

Hanes nylons

gift boxed

reinforced toe and heel,
box of 3 pairs   4.35
demi toe, box of 3 pairs   4.80
sandal foot, box of 3 pairs 5.70

from accessory collections for Mother's Day

Mindlins

on the plaza

The iridescent, jeweled butterfly
by Schreiner was advertised in
1962.

Displaced Sudeten German glass-workers resettled in parts of Austria, East Germany and West Germany. Gradually, new centers for the glass industry became established in Neugablonz, near Kaufbeuren in Bavaria; in Schwabish Gemuend in Wuerttenberg; and in the area of Linz, Austria. Generally, these glass workers came without tools or materials but with their skills and pride they rebuilt an industry. New jewelry was made and sold throughout the countryside. Gradually, better tools and materials were made and bought with the help of many individuals and governments. Exports from Austria and Neugablonz increased to the United States in 1948 [Hoffer, p.48], and helped to compensate for the limited shipping from Bohemia.

In the United States in the late 1940's, direct-selling organizations began to emerge. Of the organizations of this type which carried jewelry items, Sarah Coventry was the most prominent. Sold through home parties, Sarah Coventry jewelry became a huge business by the early 1970's.

1950's—The Costume Jewelry Industry Expands

In the 1950's, designers for popular, off-the-rack fashions for women took advantage of the availability of rhinestones once again and incorporated costume jewelry with rhinestones in their ad campaigns and fashion shows. The costume jewelry worked with and for the couture houses like Chanel, Schiaparelli, and Norman Norell to create designs that complemented the new clothing. Terry Albert of Schreiner Jewels in New York remembers rows of Italian seamstresses hand-sewing new clothing in the couture houses where Schreiner jewelry was being shown. The major department stores throughout the United States bought quantities of costume jewelry for their new jewelry counters. Department stores like Saks Fifth Avenue were a leading source for the retail public.

Between 1950 and 1955, stores in the United States imported increasing quantities of Austrian stones from Swarovski. [Hoffer, p.34] The Neugablonz glass at this time was not so much for glass stones as for glass buttons, glass beads and chandelier parts. In the early 1950's costume jewelry did not usually bear the mark of a jewelry designer or manufacturer. But after the first patent for a costume jewelry design was filed about 1940, other manufacturers began identifying their products with trademarks. Increased popularity bred competition, and the industry responded with safeguards.

The fluctuating fashion market dealt the rhinestone industry several set-backs. In 1956, for example, $11,500,000 worth of imitation stones.

Bracelets of colored stones and marcasites
in link designs, c. 1940s. M. Solomon

Three brooches made by Schreiner in the
mid-1960s are shown on an original drawing
for a newspaper advertisement which also
included other Schreiner designs.

were sold to the United States. By 1961, the volume had slackened to
$5 million as strings of colored glass beads—rather than set stones—
came into fashion. The industry had to adjust to these changes, and
some companies were more flexible than others. [AJM, p.18]

Plastics

In 1950, only two or three shops in Neugablonz made plastic items of
any sort, but that number grew to close to fifty in twenty years. Most of
them made some form of jewelry items, but also technical products
such as parts for radios and electronic equipment, clothes hangers,
toys and novelties were also made.

The 1960's—A Changing Market for Rhinestone Jewelry

By 1962 "there was a decided change towards the use of stones in
clasps and large pins," [Morris Berger, a New York stone dealer, AJM,
p.18] "as demand for beads is now receding to a position of lesser

importance in the industry." [T.B. Buffum, Jr., president of John F. Allen & Son, Inc. of Providence, R.I., AJM, p.18] Many companies expanded their lines to meet increased demand. Those companies that encouraged trends by developing and offering attractive innovations contributed to an upsurge in the demand for rhinestones. Many new designers entered the field, and the volume remained strong.

By the late 1960's, most costume jewelry houses of the previous generation were out of business or being run by a new generation with different ideas. As department stores were bought up by larger businesses, the buyers were concerned with the profits of the department over the quality of the goods or loyalty to their suppliers. Jewelry departments changed their goods to standardized designs, rather than the unusual, innovative styles.

Along with the corporate changes, the population moved away from manufactured costume jewelry in the 1970's toward craft and hand-made styles with natural materials. Some of the young consumers were labelled "Flower Children" because of their consistent preference for natural, non-industrial materials. In the United States, the Peace Movement in opposition to the war in Vietnam contributed to the decline in popularity for rhinestone jewelry among this same group.

With the end of the Vietnam War, the world went into a new phase of business prosperity and return to sophistication as "dress for success" predominated the popular attitude of young consumers. Therefore a

Blooming delights from Schreiner in the mid-1960s.

18

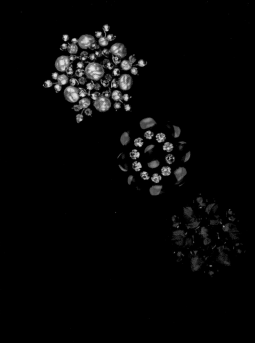

A beautiful variety of iridescent stones is combined in this group of jewelry by Regency.

Dramatic simplicity is captured in these brooches by Schreiner, c. 1960.

renewed popularity for diamond-like jewelry pervaded society and clear rhinestones once more became fashionable. New designs abounded, yet colored stones were in less demand, being used more for accents in a sea of clear rhinestones.

By the 1980's, color became important once again in jewelry, and a funny thing happened in the second-hand market. Collectors discovered costume jewelry—all over again. Once forgotten, rhinestone jewelry was given a new life as consumers went through their mothers' jewelry boxes of a generation ago, and found delight in wearing rhinestones. The designers of jewelry noticed the trend, too, so new creations were made with colored and clear rhinestones. Bright, bold, colorful rhinestone jewelry was both fashionable and collectible. The industry again flourished.

Businesses have risen and fallen over the lovely rhinestone because it has one enduring factor in its favor: it is an amazingly inexpensive copy of a precious stone. At a fraction of a cent, rhinestones emulate diamonds, sapphires, rubies, emeralds and all the rest. With rhinestones you can create an attractive ornament which can have its own unique design or be indistinguishable from its counterpart in real gemstones. With the real stones goes the aura of the precious and rare representing wealth and status. With the rhinestones go all that for everyone as well as the unique qualities of variety, availability and affordability. Rhinestones will live on.

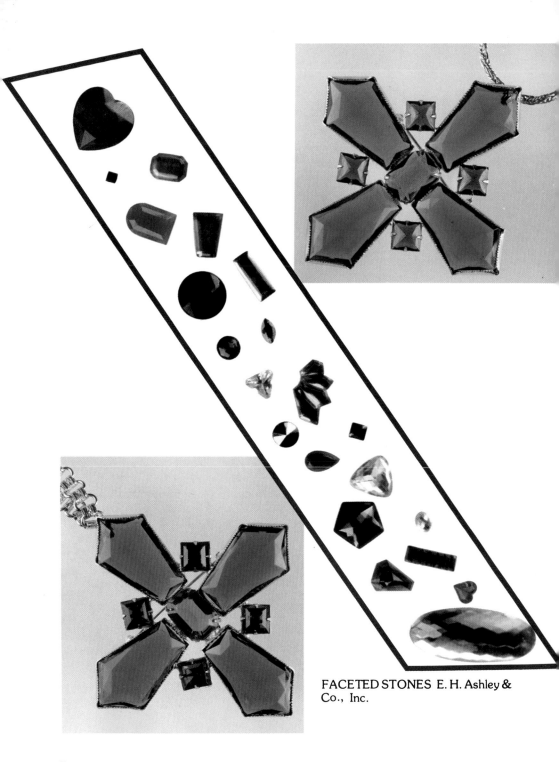

FACETED STONES E. H. Ashley & Co., Inc.

Faceted translucent stones set in two pendants by Schreiner, c. 1960.

2. Diverse shapes of rhinestones

Faceted stones

The best-selling imitation stone throughout the decades has been the round chaton cut, which is also the least expensive of the many varieties. It has eight facets and a table on the top, and eight facets coming to a point on the bottom. Chatons range in size from less than one millimeter to twelve millimeters in diameter.

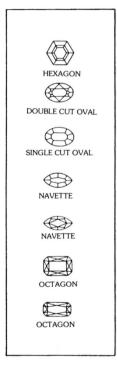

HEXAGON

DOUBLE CUT OVAL

SINGLE CUT OVAL

NAVETTE

NAVETTE

OCTAGON

OCTAGON

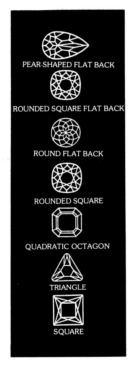

PEAR-SHAPED FLAT BACK

ROUNDED SQUARE FLAT BACK

ROUND FLAT BACK

ROUNDED SQUARE

QUADRATIC OCTAGON

TRIANGLE

SQUARE

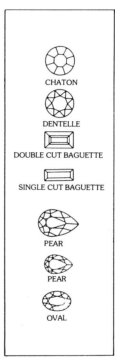

CHATON

DENTELLE

DOUBLE CUT BAGUETTE

SINGLE CUT BAGUETTE

PEAR

PEAR

OVAL

ROUND FLAT BACK

SINGLE CUT SQUARE

MARCASITE

EYESHAPE

S—SHAPE

EGGSHAPE

BELLSHAPE

HEARTSHAPE

HEARTSHAPE

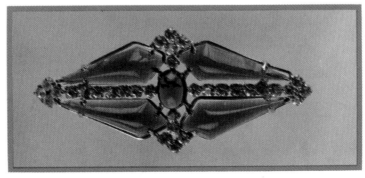

Diverse shaped stones create a dynamic
pin from Schreiner

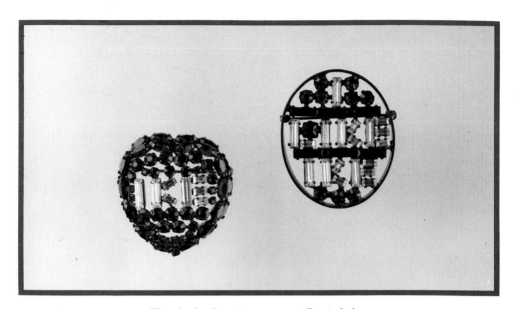

The shadowbox pin was specially made for Elizabeth Arden with faceted rhinestones spelling "I LIKE IKE." The heart-shaped pin with faceted stones spelling "IKE" was made for Mamie Eisenhower and a Republican party fund raiser; both were made by Schreiner c. 1957.

Brooch and two pair of earclips made entirely with faceted stones by Schreiner, c. 1965.

Diverse faceted stones have been set in designs as different as Victorian sweetness and stream-lined modern. The purple tones were especially popular in the mid-1960s. Marquise faceted stones are featured in this group marked *Judy Lee*.

Doublets

Before the turn of the twentieth century, a method was found to make cut glass stones more desirable. A sliver of garnet fused to the melted glass table on a stone before cutting gave the surface enough strength to withstand scratches by dust for a long time. The garnet loses its red color when it is cut so thin, so that it has been used to imitate not only colored gemstones, but diamonds as well. Known as "doublets," these stones can look pure white, even though they have a red table. Tintable doublets also became available from Neugablonz by 1950.

Lizard, lobster and turtle brooches set
with faceted stones, c. 1960.

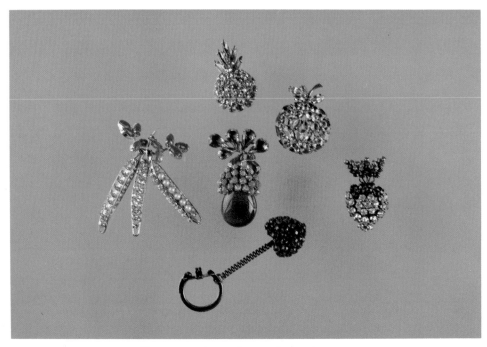

Opaque and translucent faceted stones
entirely make up the designs of these
brooches and jeweled key ring of fruit and
vegetable shapes from the 1970s made by
Schreiner.

The shaded blue faceted stones of the
brooch are designed in a swirling pattern.
The necklace of pale green faceted stones
is elegant in its simplicity. Both are marked
Sherman.

CABOCHONS E. H. Ashley & Co., Inc.

Cabochons

Large cabochon stones give form to these brooches by Schreiner, c. 1960.

Blue cabochons float on a wave of faceted stones in these earclips.

Cabochons and fine metalwork were combined by Schreiner to create these belt clasps in the 1960s.

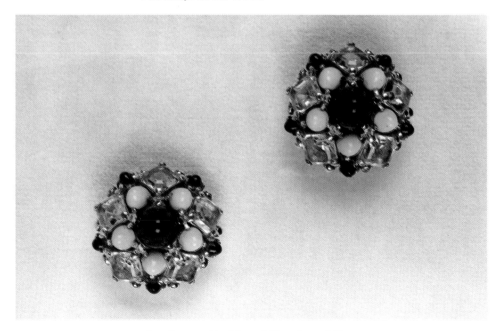

Jewelry master Marcel Boucher of New York designed these elegant earclips with blue cabochons c. 1960.

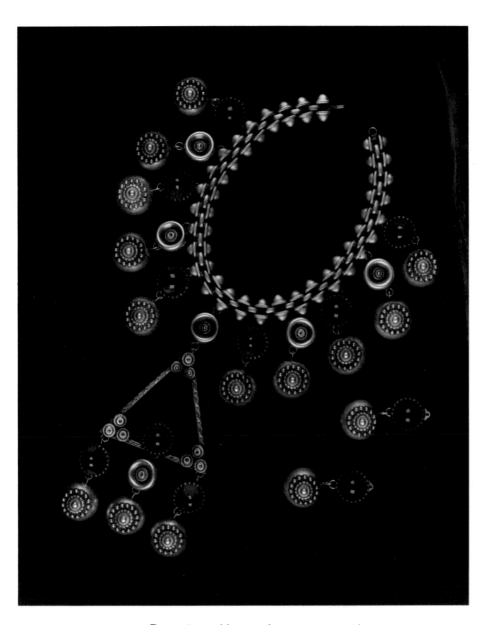

Dynamic necklace and earrings set with
large cabochons and made by Joseff of
Hollywood in 1963 for the movie
"Cleopatra."

Jeweled "Maltese Cross" pendant necklace and matching drop earrings of German glass cabochons and Austrian beads, designed by R.F. Clark, c. 1968 for Wm. de Lillo USA. Wm. de Lillo Archive.

Jeweled necklace "Geometric Tie" hand-constructed with metal tubing and German glass high domed cabochons, designed by R. F. Clark c. 1969-70 for Wm. de Lillo USA. Wm. de Lillo Archive..

Cabochons are held in magnificent metalwork settings on this jewelry by Swoboda
of California, c. 1970. Fior

PENDANTS & DROPS E. H. Ashley &
Co., Inc.

Opposite page:
Pendant stones anchor the butterfly
designs in these necklaces by Schreiner, c.
1962.

Pendants and drops

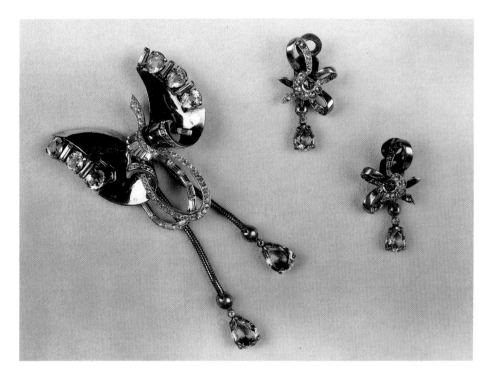

Such a fancy design by Mazer for a brooch and earclip featuring bows, clear rhinestones and aqua pendant tear drops.

The pendants create a fringe of lovely color for this necklace by Schreiner, c. 1960.

Matching bracelet and dramatic earrings which were designed by Schreiner specifically to emphasize the motion of the pendant stones.

Tear-drop faceted stones are mounted as
a pendant fringe flanking the central
composite group in this lovely necklace by
Schreiner, c. 1965.

The iridescent stones are mounted as cascading pendants on this magnificent necklace by Schreiner while the matching eardrops add a complementary design to the set.

Openwork metal supports the pendant chains and drops of this brooch marked "Kandell and Marcus, New York."

A jeweled bib necklace made with antique Czechoslovakian glass jet stones, Swarovski rondelles, and Austrian crystal faceted beads and faceted jet drops. The design was made in c. 1968-69 by R. F. Clark for Wm. de Lillo USA as a dramatic presentation of these contrasting materials, and was extended to the design of the matching drop earrings. Wm. de Lillo Archive.

Of modern design, this set of matching bracelet and earrings of decorated fabric and trims with pendant drop pearls was designed by the French firm LeSage.

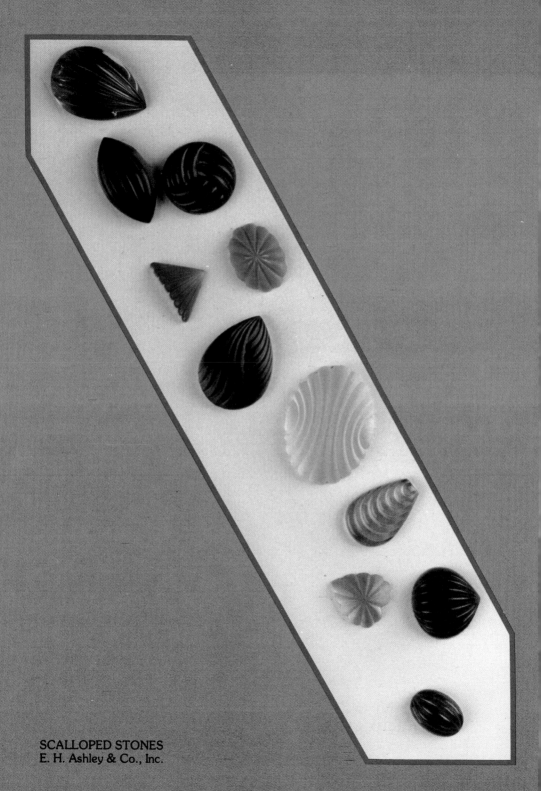

SCALLOPED STONES
E. H. Ashley & Co., Inc.

Scalloped stones

The scalloped stones add texture to the butterfly wings on this delicate and beautiful brooch designed by R. F. Clark, c. 1970 for Wm. de Lillo USA. Wm. de Lillo Archive.

Earrings made with scalloped, leaf-shaped stones and iridescent facet-cut rhinestones, marked "Lisner," c. 1960.

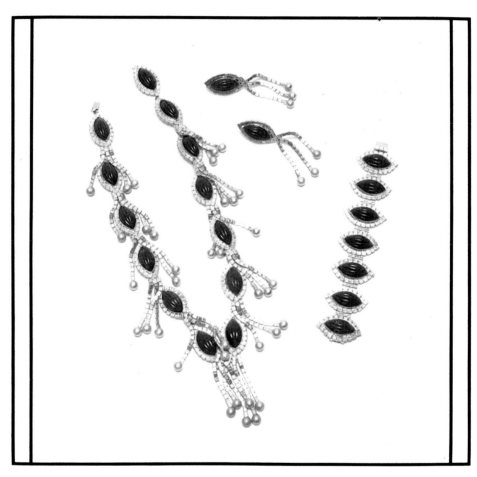

A magnificent set of jewelry featuring
scalloped German glass marquise stones
in a necklace with fringe, a hinged bracelet
and drop earrings, c. 1970-71, designed by
R. F. Clark for Wm. de Lillo USA. Wm. de
Lillo Archive

Brooch which combines two different styles of scalloped stones in a lovely wreath design, c. 1960, by Schreiner.

Two cross-shaped brooches featuring custom-designed scalloped stones mounted with facet-cut stones in pleasing colors, c. 1960, by Schreiner.

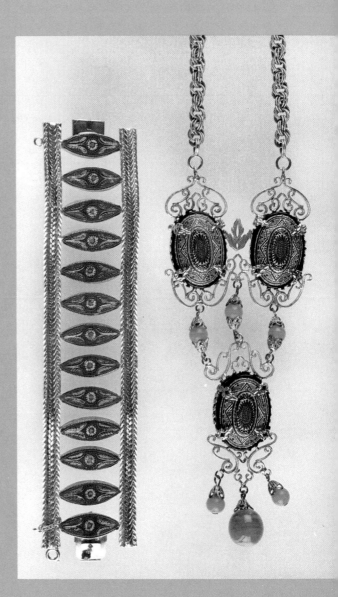

UNIQUE DESIGNS
E. H. Ashley & Co., Inc.

The highly ornamented stones in this jewelry were made in press molds where the glass was formed and the pattern applied. Pigment colors were then applied by hand to each tiny section of the design to bring out its details. The jewelry was designed and made by Schreiner in the 1960s.

Unique designs

Cameos are specially designed to replicate hard stone cameos of the Classical world, and those shown here are incorporated into jewelry marked "Florenza," c. 1960.

Pair of earrings made with custom-designed leaf-shaped opaque glass stones and iridescent round, facet-cut stones. The earrings are marked "Triad," c. 1965.

These custom-shaped stones have become the central design elements of the jewelry Grosse of Germany designed for Christian Dior. The green stone earrings were made in 1959, the pendant necklace with gold chain tassels in 1960. Fior

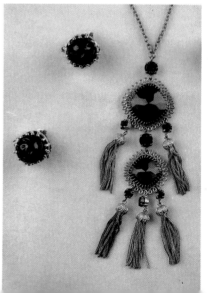

The carved and painted stones with small
floral patterns were hand made in Austria
and incorporated with Austrian blue stones
in this bracelet and two brooches from the
late 1950s. None of the pieces is marked by
a maker.

Millifiori glass was custom made and cut into octagonal stones in the 1960s for this brooch by Schreiner. The millifiori technique is associated with Venetian glass makers, and has been used in trade beads from there for hundreds of years. Its use in jewelry is very unusual.

Blue crystal has been cut and faceted into the heart, star and tear-drop shapes and then engraved to create these highly individual stones.

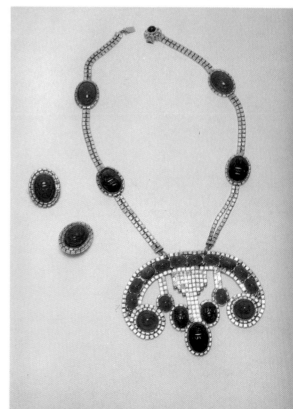

Opposite:
The leaf- and floral-shaped rhinestones were inspired by carved gems from the 1920s. Trifari was particularly adept at incorporating them into intricate designs for costume jewelry.

The red and green carved scarab stones have been carefully incorporated into this necklace design with a beautifully detailed scroll medallion, and complementary ear-clips designed by R. F. Clark , c. 1970 for Wm. de Lillo USA. Wm. de Lillo Archive.

Opposite page:
The round white stones are highly decorated with interior floral designs which create an unusual snowflake appearance. This lovely fringe necklace, with ear clips and pendant ear drops to match, was made by Schreiner, c. 1960.

SPECIAL EFFECTS E. H. Ashley & Co., Inc.

Special effects

The Aurora Borealis special effect was first popularized in 1953. One dealer has described Aurora Borealis as "the most revolutionary development since the invention of the glass cutting machine in the last century." [AJM, p.22] Its manufacturing process includes vacuum-plating of metal onto glass. The first experiments for this process were made before the second world war at the New York offices of the Josef Riedel firm of Gablonz, Czechoslovakia. Several microscopic layers of different materials on the backs of clear stones produced an interference of light and gave a varied rainbow appearance. After the war, the Riedel firm continued to make some of these iridescent stones fir the Paris market. By 1953, and only gradually at first, they came to be in demand and variations were made. Those with iridescent coatings on the tops of the stones became known as Aurora Borealis. Other metallic coatings, generally applied to the backs of the stones, produced color effects known as Volcano; light, medium, and dark Vitrail; Bermuda Blue; and Heliotrope. The machines to produce these effects were subsequently used elsewhere, including in Austria and Neugablonz.

The vacuum-plating process developed for Aurora Borealis stones was used in experiments which resulted in creating a dark grey, mirrored surface similar to real hematite. Since the late 1950's, imitation hematite has been a standard style of fancy rhinestones. Further experimentation with vacuum-plating enabled workers to make gold-finished stones. Later, gold vacuum-plating was used in conjunction with cut and tumbled processes to produce a wide variety of special effects. The discovery of the vacuum-plating process was a great innovation for the rhinestone industry.

The iridescent effect of the rhinestones adds a pleasing dimension to the floral clusters of this hair ornament made in the early 1960s by Schreiner.

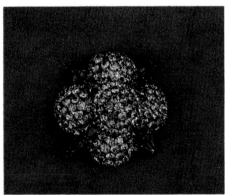

Aurora Borealis clustered stones in five domes are divided by four amethyst-colored points on this brooch by Warner, c. 1959.

This garland of iridescent rhinestones and gold toned wire is marked *Keyes*.

The Aurora Borealis effect is displayed on rhinestones of many different shapes in this jewelry. The round brooch and earclips are marked "DODDZ," the red brooch with two pear shaped stones is marked "Czechoslovakia," and the dark pink earrings are unmarked, all c. 1960.

A wreath is formed with Aurora Borealis stones mounted in prong-settings and rondells of blue tinted rhinestones for this brooch by Warner.

Deep, conical, faceted stones of blue and pink tones and an iridized surface are clustered to form this brooch. The ball drop earrings of light blue rhinestones are marked "Vogue" and date from the late 1950s.

More glittering oval domed stones, now in soft shades of green, yellow and white, are mixed with pastel faceted rhinestones to create the fringe necklace and drop earrings by Schreiner, c. 1965.

This brooch and earrings set by Florenza displays two types of stones with special effects. The oval domed stones have glittering interior particles and the teardrop shaped stones are vacuum processed for an iridescent appearance.

The faceted and dark iridescent rhinestones are mounted in this group as a bracelet, link belt, buckle for a metal cord belt and drop earrings by Schreiner, c. 1965.

Rhinestone butterflies sparkle with
iridescence in the pendant necklace by
Regency and two unmarked brooches.

A butterfly brooch by Weiss and two link
bracelets display different colorings of
iridescent stones as the dominant design
elements.

The unusual iridescent stones and gold roping of this bracelet indicate the fine workmanship with which it was made by Vendome. The brooch with translucent, prong-set rhinestones and the brooch with opaque cabochons by Vendome also incorporate fine metal elements which are important features of their designs.

The largest rhinestones in this pin and earring set are not only beautifully colored and iridescent, but are also domed, made with scalloped edges, and are pierced at the centers.

Opposite:
Four-strand bead necklace with
festoons by Coppola & Toppo, Italy.
Hinged cuff with enamel and opaque
stones including a scarab by Hattie
Carnegie. E. & J. Rothstein Antiques.

54

Beads

Beads have enjoyed a particular popularity in fashion circles for hundreds of years. A renewal occurred in 1960 and 1961 when the glass stone market was overflowing with small beads of relatively poor quality glass from diverse sources in Bohemia, Czechoslovakia, and Austria. Their relative low cost from high volume made strings of beads popular ornaments for jewelry for all classes of people—especially young women who could find in beads a diversity of ornament at affordable prices. This group of the population was the large, maturing group from the Baby Boom years of 1945-1950. Teens and adolescents loved beads. Ad campaigns showed beads as fashion accessories, sewn onto sweaters and dresses and coats in profusion. Little new store-set jewelry was needed when the beads were so much in demand. After a few years, however, "demand for beads ... reced(ed) to a position of lesser importance in the industry." [T.B. Buffum, Jr., president of John F. Allen & Son, Inc. of Providence, R.I., AJM, p.18] Always available on the market, beads can be used as accents or for major designs because they can be cleverly worked into all popular jewelry forms.

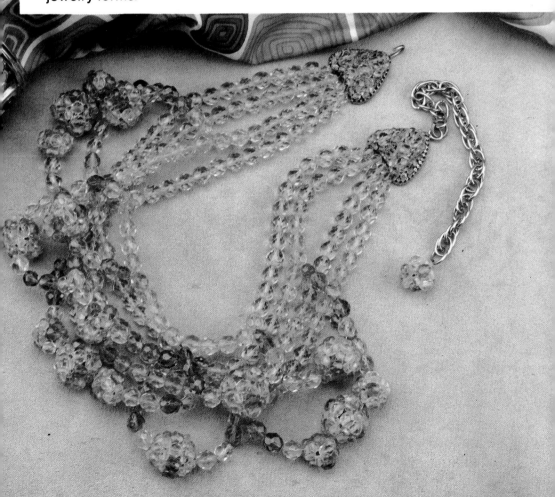

A three-strand clear crystal bead necklace designed by Adolfo for Joseph Mazer in 1977. The two beaded coil cuff bracelets are unmarked. The black beaded, flat bracelet is marked "Western Germany," c. 1960. Fior

Intricate cane beads from Eastern Europe have been attached to this silver link bracelet and earrings in an unusual and pretty arrangement.

Colorful faceted beads have been made in many shapes throughout the twentieth century.

Green and black iridescent faceted beads were popular and made by the thousands in Bohemia and Austria in the early 1960s.

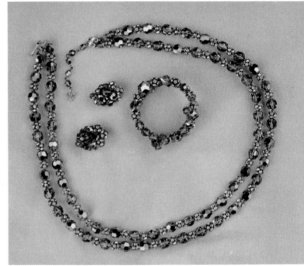

A choker necklace and matching bracelet of faceted red beads are beautifully accented with clear rhinestones and a gold setting with square stones in a fresh design by R.F. Clark, c. 1970 for Wm. de Lillo USA. Wm. de Lillo Archive

Coppola & Toppo of Italy created these elaborate bead necklaces and ear clips of distinction. E. & J. Rothstein Antiques.

Faceted iridescent beads and cluster rhinestones are combined to create this glittering set by Vendome.

Opposite page:
Tiny seed and bugle beads of colored glass and sequins are used by Le Sage of Paris to construct contemporary jewelry of innovative designs. The variety is delightful and these always start a conversation among the admirers.

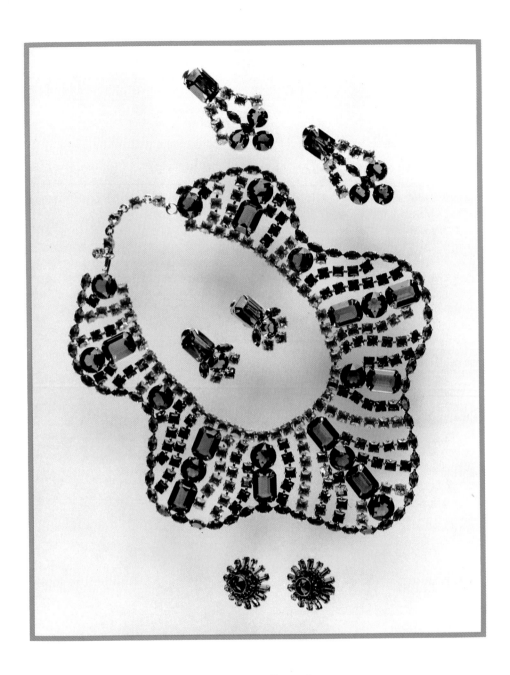

A brilliant necklace designed by Schreiner and made entirely with translucent colored glass rhinestones set in prongs, c. 1960. The three pair of matching earrings each complement the necklace without competing with its dramatic impact.

Opposite page:
Hang your wish on a star. These brooches include both foiled and unfoiled clear rhinestones which sparkle variously as they catch light and thereby produce the twinkling appearance the designer sought. They were made by Schreiner in the 1960s.

3. Rhinestones in a spectrum of colors

Clear—
diamond, crystal, white topaz

Diamonds are a pure form of crystallized carbon, perfectly clear and harder than any other material. When cut and polished to enhance their innate reflecting properties, diamonds are brilliant like no other substance. Substitutes for diamonds in natural substances have been poor by comparison. Natural rock crystal is softer and far less brilliant. White sapphire, white topaz and white spinel have not been available in sufficient volume to be important. Even glass cut to simulate diamonds usually has been too soft so that it becomes scratched and dulled. Much of the common abrasive dust which scratches materials when it is wiped off is quartz dust, and anything softer than quartz will become readily worn and scratched.

Glass substitutes for diamonds have been a challenge to the jewelry industry throughout the twentieth century. In the late 1940's, imitation diamonds were produced from strontium titanate, a completely man-made substance not found in nature. These stones look even more brilliant than diamond and throw back to the viewer a rich display of colors. The first of these stones were yellowish, but later were refined

to pure white. They were popular in good jewelry stores for many years. Because the substance is very soft, it wore away quickly. A subsequent refinement was the use of a strontium titanate back cemented to a harder white spinel or white sapphire front.

Ytrium-aluminum-garnet, known popularly as "yag," was a diamond replica of less brilliance and less cost than the strontium titanate. In the 1980's, cubic zirconia came on the market as a diamond substitute, and it seems to possess the requisite hardness and brilliance.

Crystal necklace of German frosted, square, high-domed, foiled cabochon rhinestones hand mounted in 18k gold electro-plated metal with smooth, frosted crystal German beads, designed by R.F. Clark, c. 1970, for Wm. de Lillo USA. Wm. de Lillo Archive

Jeweled ruffle necklace made with Swarovski crystal faux diamonds and clear Austrian crystal, faceted square rhinestones by R.F. Clark, c. 1969, for Wm. de Lillo USA. Wm. de Lillo Archive.

A magnificent clear and colored stone brooch by Schreiner is displayed with an advertisement for others of similar designs from a newspaper of the mid-1960s.

Clear, emerald cut, Swarovski rhinestones and lovely clear Austrian crystal beads are combined with 18kt gold plated settings in this "Pineapple" necklace designed by R. F. Clark, c. 1969, for Wm. de Lillo USA. Wm. de Lillo Archive.

Tiaras of simple design or the most queenly creation were popular accompaniments to formal fashions in the 1950-60 era.

The fluid ribbon design of this unmarked brooch is accented with clear rhinestones in a beautiful openwork pattern. The nearly-matching earrings are marked "Trifari."

Small faux diamonds carry out the plant designs on these two brooches by Jomaz from the 1960s. The green stones are carved as individual leaves.

A group of small accent brooches from c. 1963, all with clear faux diamond rhinestones. The scissors and musical note are marked "Pell." The design with green cabochons is marked "Ciro," and the remaining four brooches are each marked "Polcini." Fior

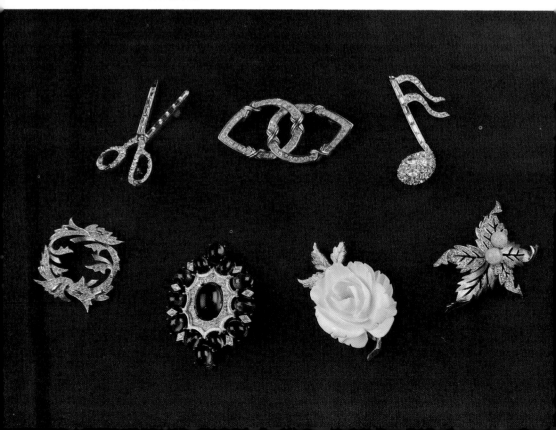

The beautiful clear Austrian stones are the most important components of these brooches and earrings by Eisenberg from the 1960s.

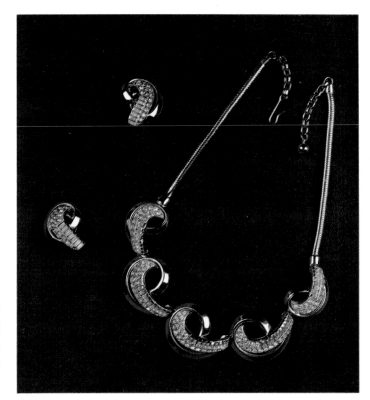

Clear rhinestones and silver are sculpted in crescent links for this choker and matching ear-clips by Schia-parelli, early 1950s.

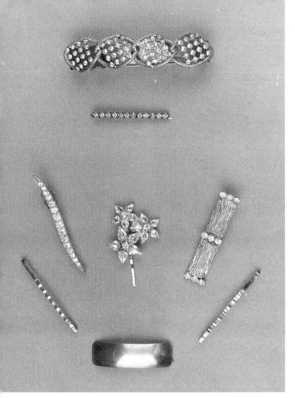

Hair ornaments with rhinestones make lovely accents. These examples are unmarked and date from the 1950-60 era. F. Cronin

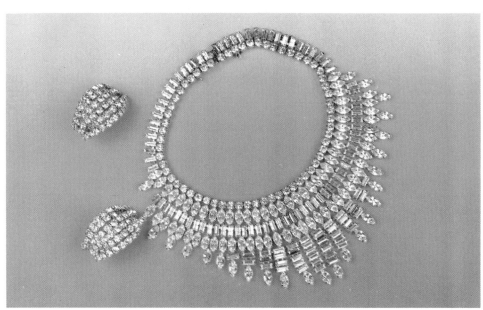

The marquis, round and baguette clear rhinestones are arranged in a formal cascading design on this exquisite necklace and the earclips have staggered lines of rhinestones. Both are unmarked. F. Cronin

A pendant brooch with drop pearl and matching earclips of openwork and pave clear rhinestones by Schreiner from the 1960s.

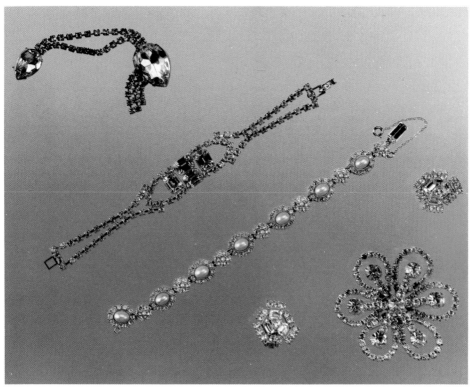

The clear rocks and rhinestones in this group of jewelry define the designs. The bracelet with pearls is signed "Ciner" and the earrings are signed "Bogoff," while the remaining pieces are unmarked.

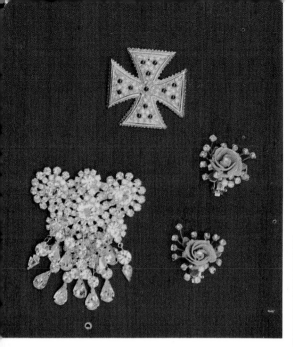

Hattie Carnegie made each of these designs which demonstrate the diversity of this company. The clear rhinestones, however, are used effectively in each, from the formal Maltese Cross design, to the flamboyant girandole style brooch, and the whimsical earclips with water droplets-- all made with rhinestones!

Huge clear rhinestones are individually mounted with prongs for earclips.

Un-foiled rhinestones of emerald and round shapes are clustered on crescents for these earclips.

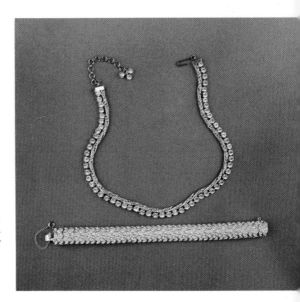

Clear rhinestones and gold define the opulent appearance of these designs in a link bracelet by Ciner and a choker necklace by Hattie Carnegie.

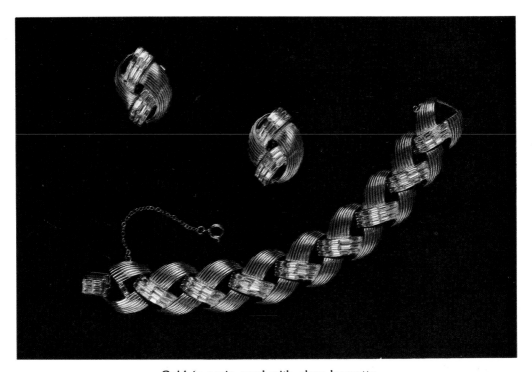

Gold is again used with clear baguette rhinestones for this interesting braided design in a bracelet and earclips by Coro.

The stunning bird brooch is a classic demonstration of Marcel Boucher's brilliant design sense. His use of clear rhinestones complements the overall design by creating a rough texture of ruffled feathers.

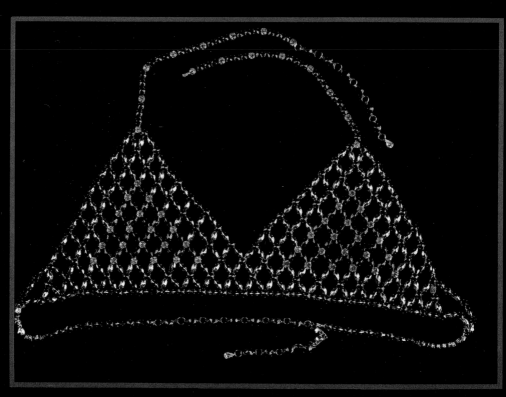

A novel ornament, this rhinestone halter top was custom designed and made in only very limited quantity by Schreiner in the 1960s.

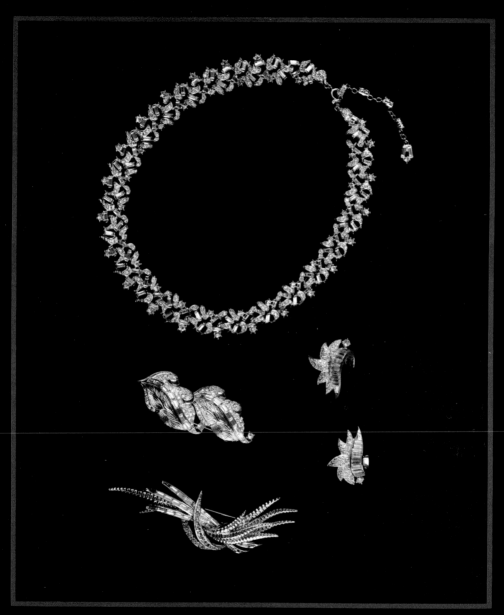

The fine openwork and rhinestone link
necklace was made by Attwood and
Sawyer c. 1970. The double leaf clips are
by Coro Duette, while the ear clips are
marked *Jomaz*. The fine brooch below is
by Carven, designed by Gonthiez Freres,
c. 1975. Fior

The full rhinestone ball necklace is a superior example of this style popularized in the 1920s. The earrings complement the necklace by remaining simplistic in design, yet the materials are of the best quality.

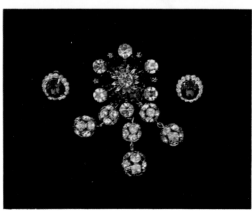

The rhinestone ball drops are suspended from a star-like brooch with clear and amethyst rhinestones and the earrings are complementary in design.

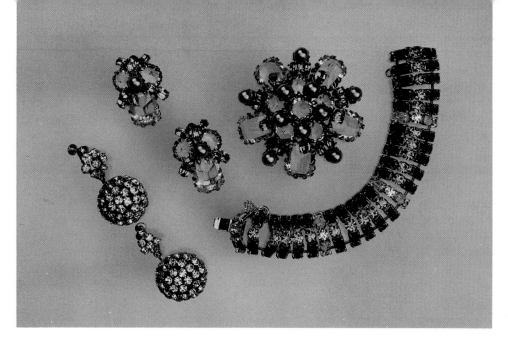

The rhinestone ball drop earrings by Schreiner date from the 1940s. The parure of brooch, bracelet and earrings combine clear, unfoiled emerald-cut stones with grey stones and grey pearls to create an unusual set that is very effective for evening wear. This jewelry was made by Schreiner in the 1960s.

The choker necklace combines graduated rhinestone balls, unusual clustered crystal and iridescent faceted beads. The rhinestone ball drop earrings are the perfect accompaniment!

This fascinating necklace has rhinestone cluster beads combined with clear and iridescent beads and rondelles. The earrings are marked "Vogue."

Clear, unfoiled stones are the predominant elements in this dynamic jewelry by Schreiner from the 1960s. Because background colors show through the clear glass, the jewelry interacts with the clothing it accompanies.

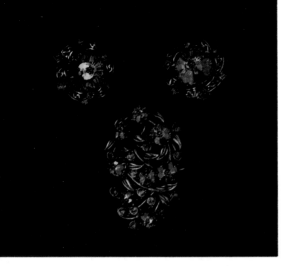

Blue stones form the flowerheads for the bouquets in this pin and earclips set by Hollycraft.

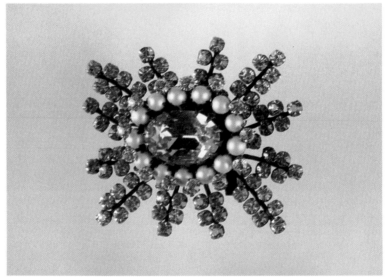

Sky blue, clear and iridescent rhinestones with pearl accents make a shimmering snowflake brooch by Schreiner, c. 1965.

The open design of this pin and earclips set gives depth to the individually set blue and clear rhinestones.

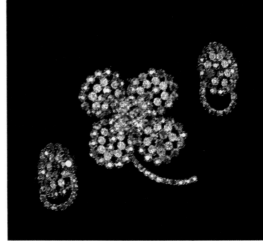

Blue—
sapphire, turquoise, aquamarine, lapis lazuli

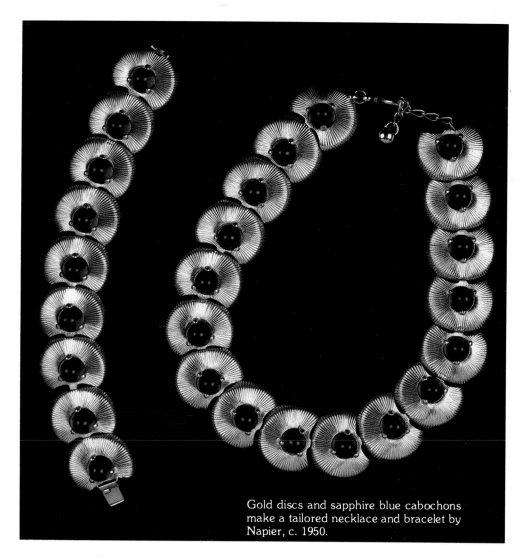

Gold discs and sapphire blue cabochons make a tailored necklace and bracelet by Napier, c. 1950.

Sapphires

The first synthetic sapphire was successfully produced about 1910 from the same elements as natural sapphire. Once the chemistry was understood, sapphire could be manufactured in blue as well as clear and yellow colors. The synthetic sapphire was much harder than glass or rock crystal. Later, synthetic spinels were produced as well, being softer, but more brilliant than synthetic sapphire.

In the late 1940's, the growing industry in Neugablonz produced star sapphires with the floating star.

These striking designs in blue and gold have a classic and timeless quality of conservative good taste. They all were designed by R. F. Clark for Wm. de Lillo USA and exemplify the restrained craftsmanship of excellent designers. Wm. de Lillo Archive.

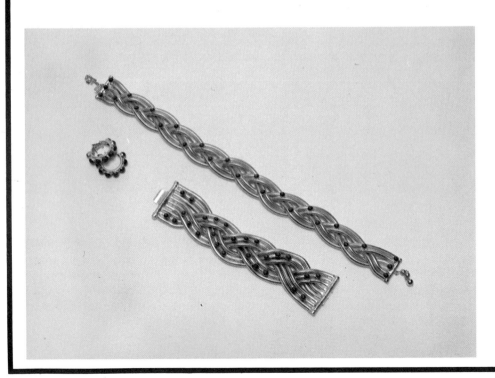

A multitude of blue shades is combined in this delicate brooch design by Schreiner

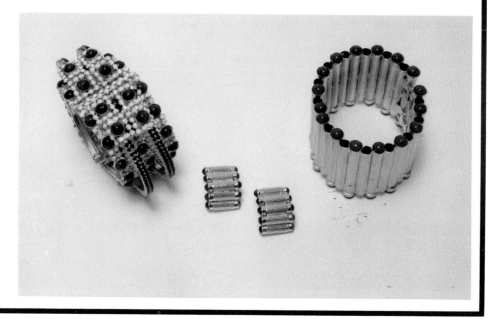

The shapes of the stones themselves are important features of this jewelry by Schreiner. In the construction of these brooches and earrings, the success of the designs is achieved only by the careful balance of shapes, colors and craftsmanship.

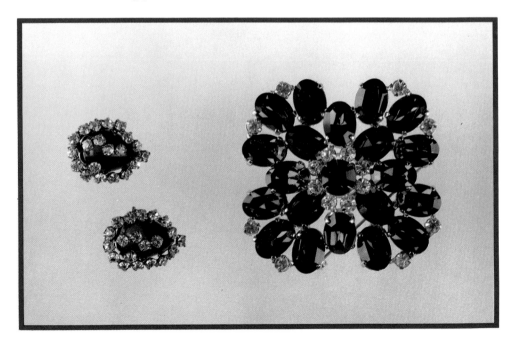

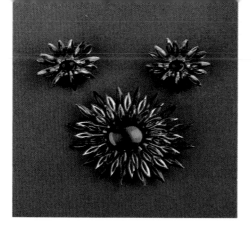

The sapphire blue of the cabochons in this pin and earring set by Trifari is repeated in the enameling of the petals of the floral settings.

Pointed opaque blue stones burst from a colorful rhinestone center in this brooch by Schreiner.

Pear-shaped, sapphire blue stones balance the design of this magnificent bar pin by Schreiner

This fine set of jewelry by Weiss combines blue stones of varying shades with strong lineal design shapes which are characteristic of styles so popular in the late 1950s and 1960s.

81

The pretty, leaf pattern, link necklace and
the earclips were made by Trifari. The fine
openwork leaf brooch with a rhinestone fly
is unmarked.

Cornflower blue rhinestones are featured in this bouquet brooch with ribbon tie.

Deep sapphire blue marquis and light blue chaton rhinestones are combined in this unmarked pin and earclips.

Gold pendant earrings by Schreiner of fine openwork segments studded with light blue chatons.

Unfoiled blue rhinestones bring depth to the design of this trembling butterfly brooch poised above a delicate floral rhinestone brooch, both by Schreiner, c. 1965.

Blue trapezoids and graduated round stones are each linked and set with prongs in these necklaces from the 1950s.

Deep blue rhinestones predominate the designs of these bracelets and pin by Kramer of New York, c. 1950s.

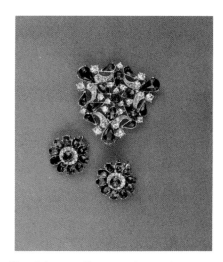

The delicacy of lace is achieved by varying the shapes and sizes of the blue stones, and combining them with openwork and clear chatons. This brooch and earclips were designed by Bogoff.

A wonderful tiered, flexible necklace of electroplated 18kt gold and antique Czechoslovakian crystal faux emerald and sapphire stones has a fringe of frosted crystal, pear-shaped drops and is framed with Swarovski crystal faux diamonds. This fantastic design was made by R. F. Clark, c. 1969-70 for Wm. de Lillo USA. Wm. de Lillo Archive.

Aqua blue shimmers in the facets of this uniquely shaped rhinestone mounted with colored marquis and chaton stones above an enormous pearl drop. This design by Schreiner, c. 1960, is bold and lovely.

Turquoise and sapphire blue rhinestones are mounted in gold colored settings for this diverse group of brooches and earrings by Carven. Fior

A dramatic articulated mobile necklace by R. F. Clark was made entirely by hand methods, c. 1970 for Wm. de Lillo USA, with rare antique Czechoslovakian faux zircon crystal stones and Swarovski "Comet Or" stones. Wm. de Lillo Archive.

This "spoke pin" by Schreiner was made in "tones of amethyst, topaz, emerald, marcasite or crystal" as well as in blue and sold originally, in the 1960s, for ten dollars.

The soft tones of turquoise are featured in these brooches and pendant by Schreiner from the 1960s.

A massive collar of solid rhinestones designed to resemble fine lace with emerald insets is magnificent. The only possible accompaniment is the emerald tone brooch shown above. Both pieces were made by Schreiner, c. 1960s.

Green—
jade, emerald

A regal pendant brooch, of beautifully sculpted gold electroplated settings, featuring emerald green cabochons and clear chatons, was designed by R. F. Clark, c. 1968 for Wm. de Lillo USA. Wm. de Lillo Archive.

Faceted emerald green and clear rhinestones are featured in this classic style matching set by Hattie Carnegie, c. 1960.

Emerald colored baguettes and graduated clear marquis stones were cleverly arranged to form a stunning leaf brooch by Schreiner, c. 1960.

Emerald cut green rhinestones are isolated on a lyre-shaped gold backing in these handsome ear clips from the 1950s.

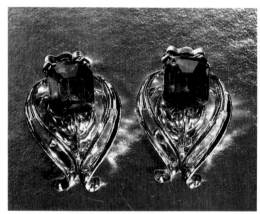

The delicate openwork link bracelet and pair of post-back ear pendants date from the 1920s when Old World craftsmanship was the pride of the jewelry industry. This group spans fifty years, for the pendant brooch and ear clips, each with bolder designs and clear chaton detailing, date from the 1970s; all are unmarked.

Long keystone shaped stones were custom made for use only by the Schreiner company from about 1950 until the late 1970s. The bold design of this brooch and matching earclips is given depth by the staggered placement of the keystone rhinestones, c. 1965.

Pear shaped peridot and aquamarine colored rhinestones are featured in this spectacular matching set designed by R. F. Clark, c. 1972 for Wm. de Lillo USA. The rhodium plated settings support Swarovski stones. This design group was inspired by the Shah of Iran's 25th anniversary party. Wm. de Lillo Archive.

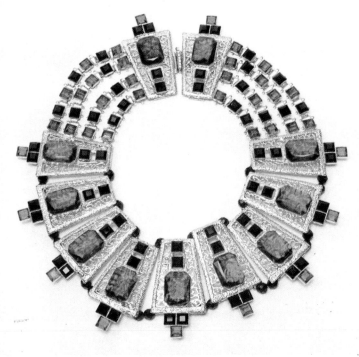

The articulated neck-lace of unfoiled, aqua and peridot, long-faceted rhinestones was hand constructed by R.F. Clark, c. 1970 for Wm. de Lillo USA. Wm. de Lillo Archive

The trapeze necklace of articulated links features faux emerald rhinestones, German crystal and jet with 18k gold electroplating. This sensational design and striking combination of materials was made, c. 1972, by R.F. Clark for Wm. de Lillo USA. Wm. de Lillo Archive

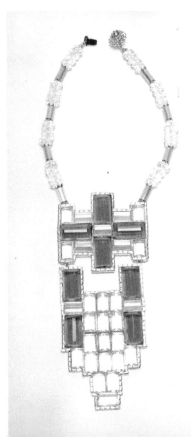

Emerald green, German crystal cabochons are held by navette shaped jeweled elements of Swarovski rhinestones and twisted wire on this elegant, hand-constructed, cushion-shaped brooch and matching earclips. They were made by R. F. Clark, c. 1968 for Wm. de Lillo USA. Wm. de Lillo Archive

Dark green beads and extraordinary clear rhinestone terminals demonstrate fine French workmanship from the 1920s in this unusual matching set which includes a necklace, a choker, two bracelets and pendant earrings. Cobra & Bellamy

Inspiration from Thailand was certainly at the root of these designs from the early 1960s. The malachite green cabochon earclips were made by Givenchy, the dramatic jade green Buddah pendant was made by Ciner, and the dangling stamped and openwork earrings are unmarked.

Peridot green rhinestones are superimposed on gold plated wire ropes in this delicate, cushion-shaped brooch by R. F. Clark, c. 1968 for Wm. de Lillo USA. The Sapphire blue cabochon has a particularly high dome. Wm. de Lillo Archive.

Carved jade green opaque stones are linked with fine gold mountings in the bracelet, and the focal point of an exquisite pendant necklace, both made by Schreiner, c. 1960.

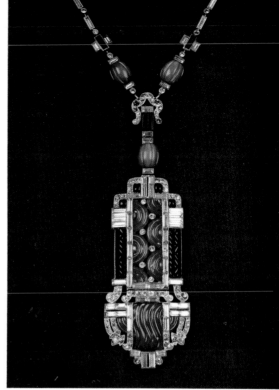

Clustered jade green grape drops cascade with naturalistic leaf designs for a pin and earring set from the 1970s.

Bangle bracelets, too, are set with rhinestones in diverse patterns. Here, the ram's head design is by Hattie Carnegie; the orange enamel hinged bracelet with emerald green pear-shaped stones is by Kenneth Jay Lane; and the fanciest one of all, covered with glass cabochons, is unmarked.

This pendant necklace design is one of the most complex attempted in costume jewelry. The unique green and black ribbed stones are highly stylized, and their arrangement, with clear baguette and chaton rhinestones, is a masterwork in the Deco style. Cobra & Bellamy

Ruby red rhinestones and fine gold toned strap-work are arranged in swirled patterns reminiscent of textile designs from Kashmir. This unmarked jewelry has exceptionally fine workmanship and probably dates from the 1930s, perhaps having been made in eastern Germany.

Deep red Bohemian crystal rhinestones and the very fine openwork metal elements are products of the Czechoslovakian mountain areas around Gablonz from the 1920s and 1930s era. While the jewelry is unmarked, its quality cannot be disputed.

Red—
ruby, garnet, carnelian

Two styles, both marked "Western Germany," represent the flexibility of an industry in transition in the 1950s. The earrings were made in the old style, perfected in Germany in the 1920s and made continuously for the next forty years at least, while the floral brooch was made with new molding techniques and plastics instead of glass.

Dress clips were popular ornaments in the 1940s and 1950s. The two single clips shown here have fine, deeply colored rhinestones probably from Austria. The double clip is a Coro Duette, c.1955.

Fluid motion is captured in rhinestones
and conveyed in these designs by
Schreiner, c. 1960.

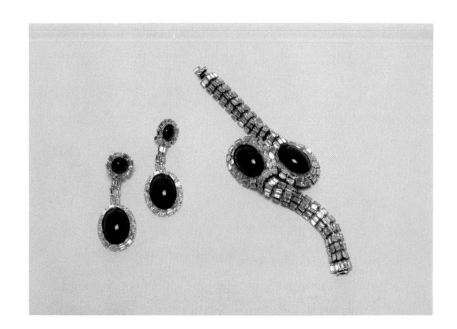

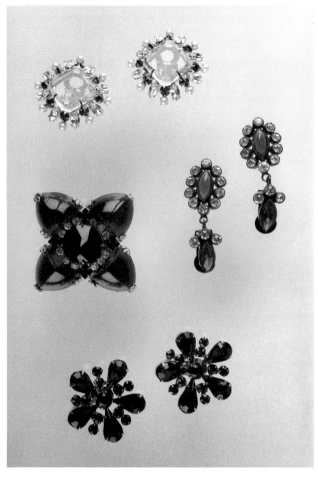

The jeweled, flexible domed bracelet and earclips are made entirely with Austrian glass mottled ruby cabochons and Swarovski faux diamond baguettes. They were designed and hand-constructed by R.F. Clark, c. 1971, for a private client of Wm. de Lillo USA. Wm. de Lillo Archive

Red rhinestones, both faceted and cabochon in shape, and ranging in color from blood red to pale pink, carry out these brooch and earring designs by Schreiner from the 1960s.

Tiny red, purple and clear chaton cut rhinestones were used for these designs by Weiss, c. 1960.

Schreiner's tulip pin was made with ruby red, yellow, white, pink or lavender rhinestones, c. 1960.

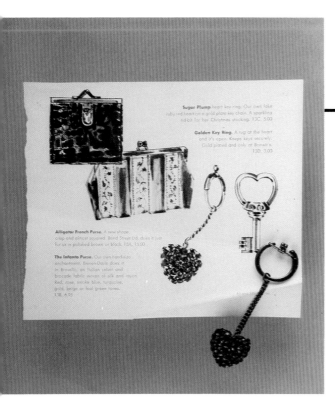

The ruby red heart key ring ornament was made by Schreiner, c. 1962.

Fashion red, prong-set rhinestones of diverse faceted shapes are used exclusively in this unmarked jewelry from the late 1950s.

Trifari's classic chain choker is set with an enormous ruby red, emerald cut stone. The coiled snake bracelet is always poised to set a striking impression.

Individually set stones and ribbons of gold plated metal make a pretty set of brooch and shadow-box ear clips by Trifari.

A large, starburst brooch, made by Schreiner with matching earclips, combines an oval faceted red stone and baguettes, 1960s.

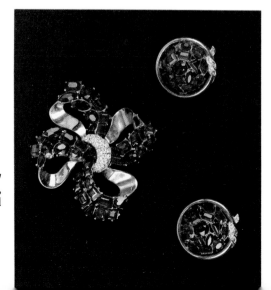

Red hearts convey sentiment in every language and in these necklace and pendant earclip designs by Schreiner from the late 1950s.

A bright red sunburst, with trailing comet tail, is made into a sparkling necklace and matching earrings.

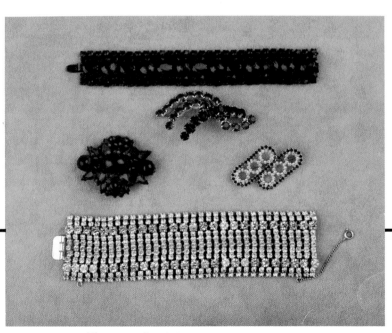

The two all-red rhinestone brooches are marked "Kramer of New York." The third brooch and two wide cuff bracelets, while beautifully made exclusively with prong-set, flexible links, are unmarked.

Apples, oranges and strawberries in molded plastic are studded with rhinestones and enameled metal stems and leaves. Only the apples are marked, by Weiss, c. 1960s.

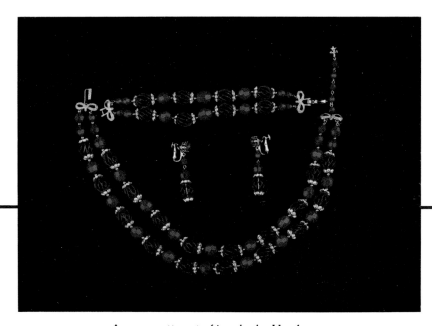

A very pretty set of jewelry by Vendome, with lots of refinement, this group includes faceted glass beads, rondelles, wirework beads and bow-knot terminals.

Pink—
rose quartz, coral

Opposite page:

Shades of pink rose quartz in jewelry by Schreiner including two large brooches and a fascinating pendant necklace with gold chain and lime-colored rhinestone accents in a shadowbox design, c. 1960.

Pink emerald cut and chaton rhinestones are artfully arranged to create a brooch and earclips from the 1950s.

Pale and very feminine, the pink stones in these large brooches and bracelet by Schreiner are beautifully enhanced by pearl, amethyst and clear rhinestones, c. 1960.

Opaque and translucent, cabochon and faceted, pink rhinestones of each variety are combined for this lovely unmarked group from the 1950s.

Pink chatons are again used to frame and accent the red, pear-shaped rhinestones in this unmarked matching set from the 1950s.

Each delicate link of this choker by Coro supports pink iridescent rhinestone pendants that sparkle as they move, c.1960.

Pear-shaped, coral-colored rhinestones and clear chatons are beautifully combined by Kenneth Jay Lane in this delicate necklace with matching pendant earclips. E. & J. Rothstein Antiques.

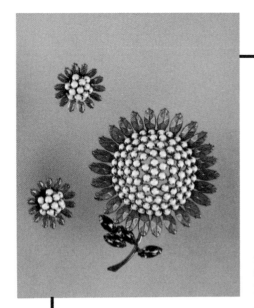

Coral red and light turquoise opaque stones are combined in this cheerful sunflower design by Schreiner from the 1960s.

What a wonderful dragonfly! The mottled pink wings dominate the design while the shaded tones are repeated in the darker eyes and body sections. The floral bouquet brooch is charming and interesting for its variety of colored stones, both opaque and translucent, set with fine gold wire work. The black wires of the third brooch certainly intensify the darker shades of rhinestones in this balanced design. All were made by Schreiner, c. 1960.

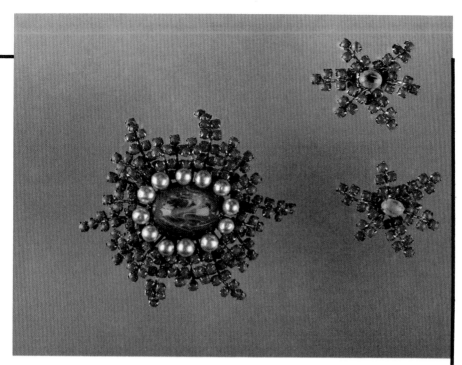

Pink coral rhinestones are featured in the
fragile-looking, open designs for these
brooches and earrings by Schreiner. The
pearl, lapis and jade-like accents add depth
which balances the designs.

Purple kite-shaped, faceted rhinestones are mixed with iridescent chatons for this unusual, unmarked, matching set of jewelry from the 1950s.

Purple—
amethyst

The pressed and gilded openwork frame is remarkably detailed around the diamond-shaped, amethyst colored rhinestone in this brooch from the 1930s.

Long and graceful drop earclips and a matching jeweled, hinged, cuff bracelet are set with Austrian faceted crystal amethyst colored stones, glass pearls and Swarovski faux diamonds. These exquisite designs were made by R. F. Clark, c. 1969-1970 for Wm. de Lillo USA. Wm. de Lillo Archive.

Large, purple, faceted rhinestones are
banded with matching chatons in the
bracelet and earclips set on the left from
the 1950s. Accompanying them are a
handsome Sarah Coventry design with
fine pierced work silver frame and large
faceted rhinestones.

The staggered arrangement of the pear-shaped purple stones gives a rotating motion to the design of this pendant by Schreiner

Pale purple rhinestones enliven the gold chain links of this unmarked bracelet from the 1950s.

Amethyst colored, faceted rhinestones of important size form the very interesting cross brooch and flowerhead brooch, both unmarked and from the 1960s.

Ivory colored petals of this cheerful daisy
brooch are carefully hand set rhinestones
around an oval cabochon center. The
design was also made by Schreiner in
coral, black, blue, yellow and rose colors,
c. 1960.

More flower brooches in ivory and
cornflower blue rhinestones by Schreiner,
c. 1960.

White—
ivory, moonstone, opal

Opals
In the early 1920's, floating opals were invented in the United States and the process to make them was patented. By 1925, jewelry with floating opals was available in jewelry stores. After a generation of dormancy, interest in these unusual stones was renewed, along with the general interest in rhinestones, around 1950. Silver opals became available from Neugablonz.

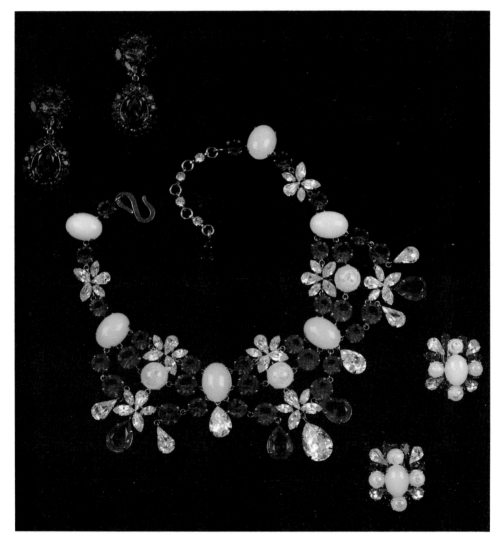

Moonstone rhinestones are aglow among faux ruby and diamond stones in this magnificent necklace, with two pairs of earclips by Christian Dior in 1959.

A jeweled pectoral necklace and matching cuff slave bracelet were hand-constructed of hammered and shaped, 18kt gold electroplated brass to encase German crystal cabochon moonstones in a forceful design by R.F. Clark, c. 1970 for Wm. de Lillo USA. Wm. de Lillo Archive

Silver scrollwork, ivory rhinestones and grey chatons are arranged in a delicate choker necklace by Lisner. The complementary brooch and earclips of emerald cut rhinestones are by Weiss.

This handsome matching set of jewelry in contrasting squares captures the beauty of ivory beads and lapis lazuli cabochons in their rhinestone counterparts in an imaginative design by R. F. Clark, c. 1968 for Wm. de Lillo USA. Wm. de Lillo Archive

White rhinestones were crafted into decorative scatter pins in 1956 by Schreiner, and shown with sophisticated garments, as in this advertisement for coats at I. Magnin & Co.

A jeweled bib of magnificent appearance created by Schreiner with black pendant baroque pearls and grey and clear rhinestones, and pendant earclips matching, c. 1960.

Grey—
Smoky topaz, diamond

Grey rhinestones in an assortment of
tones and shapes are mounted in prongs
and gold rope frames to create a dynamic
clustered brooch, c. 1965.

Opaque grey stones are framed with clear
rhinestones in this set of unmarked jewelry
from the 1950s.

Grosse of Germany designed is group of
jewelry for Christian Dior, c. 1958. The use
of grey rhinestones was considered a
subtle and rich appearance, and their
combination with gold chain links, with
grey pearls and light purple faceted
rhinestones achieves three different
effects.

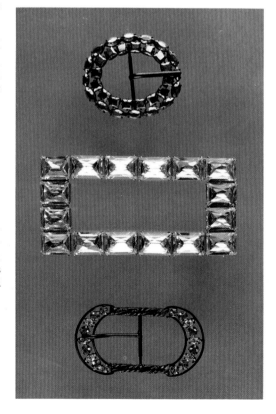

Belt buckles were an important accessory
to the couture industry and Schreiner
made these with grey and clear foil backed
rhinestones, c. 1960. The bottom buckle is
turned to show the fully encased and
prong-set stones.

Large grey and clear Austrian rhinestones comprise the swirling brooch and clustered earclips labeled "Eisenberg Ice" by the Chicago company that soared to success with these remarkable designs, c. 1965.

Jet black beads are woven together as a sophisticated choker, and then the crystal leaves are added in a profusion of light and lacy ornament to make a delightful necklace. R. F. Clark designed and constructed this necklace, c. 1968 for Wm. de Lillo USA. Wm. de Lillo Archive

These composition molded brooches and pendant were made to imitate jet in the late nineteenth century, probably in France. Pat Funt Gallery

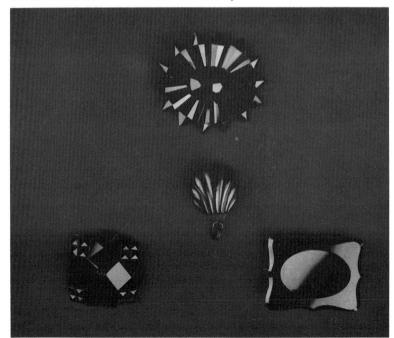

Black—
jet, onyx

The black faceted beads encircle a solid dome of clear rhinestones in this daisy-designed brooch and earrings by Vendome from the 1960s.

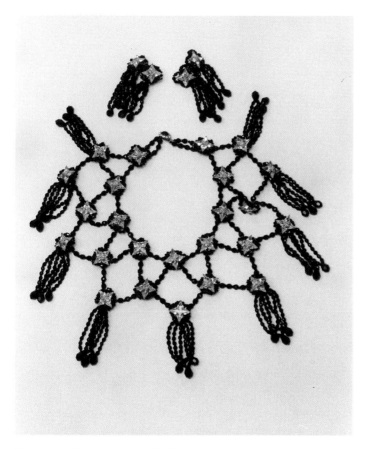

The beautiful, jeweled Trellis design necklace utilizes star-shaped centers and German glass jet beads for a lace and tassel design of great imagination. The necklace was hand-constructed by R. F. Clark, c. 1970 for Wm. de Lillo USA. Wm. de Lillo Archive

Black rhinestones and clear chaton
accents are set in prongs throughout these
designs for an unmarked matching set
from the late 1950s.

Evening jewelry designed and constructed by R. F. Clark in 1972 is shown featuring Swarovski diamante ribbon. The group includes a hinged cuff bracelet, a necklace with black silk tassels, a bowtie clip and a smaller bowtie brooch, and two styles of matching earclips: one a simple button style and one with silk tassels. Wm. de Lillo Archive

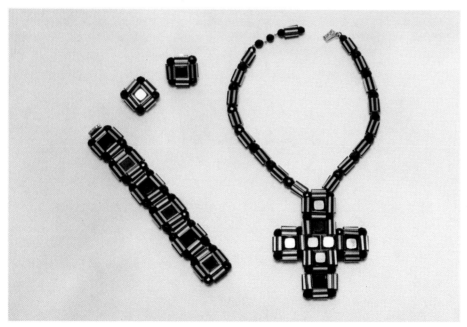

German glass hematite stones with wired black and frosted glass bagle beads have been ingeniously combined to create this dramatic matching set by R. F. Clark, c. 1970 for Wm. de Lillo USA. Wm. de Lillo Archive.

This light and particularly interesting set has a jeweled Bamboo motif of German crystal, faux topaz, faceted and cabochon stones and beads in an 18kt gold electro-plated brass mounting. The brooch, bracelet and earclips were hand constructed by R. F. Clark, c. 1969-70 for Wm. de Lillo USA. Wm. de Lillo Archive

The jeweled abstract flower brooch and earclips are constructed with Swarovski crystal faceted faux topaz stones, set and soldered in 18kt gold electroplated bezels, and faux diamond rosettes. They were designed and made in 1973 by R. F. Clark, for Wm. de Lillo USA. Wm. de Lillo Archive

Yellow and Brown—
amber, topaz, citrine

Amber cabochon rhinestones are featured in this gorgeous pendant necklace by Schreiner from about 1964. The shaded yellow lines of amber are emphasized by contrasting them with green and clear faceted stones and a geometric design.

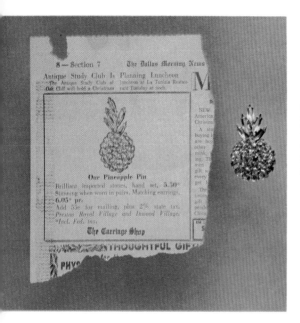

Schreiner's Pineapple Pin was featured in an advertisement in the Dallas Morning News in the early 1960s. The citrine yellow chatons and pale green marquis rhinestones cleverly represent the rough texture and form of a pineapple.

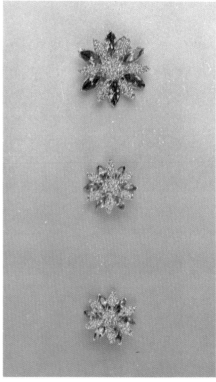

Citrine yellow chatons are again chosen with pale green marquis rhinestones for this brooch and earclips star design from the early 1960s.

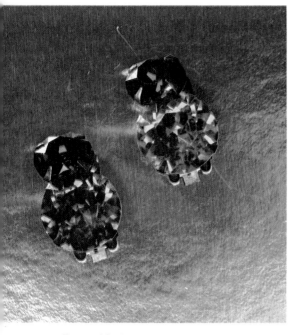

Big and bold, just two magnificent topaz rhinestones set in prongs for earclips.

Light and feathery, the brooch is set with marquis and round topaz and iridescent rhinestones, and is marked "Austria." The earclips perfectly complement the design and are unmarked.

Citrine yellow and topaz brown rhinestones are woven together in this lacy design for a magnificent matching set whose designer is unknown, c. 1965.

Elsa Schiaparelli whimsically designed a rhinestone frog to rest on this gold leaf brooch and combined a really interesting assortment of special stones for the earclips. The detail in these designs is worth a long and careful investigation.

Beads of dark and yellow amber, clear crystal, and white glass were very fashionable in 1959 when Grosse of Germany designed these necklaces for Christian Dior. Above is the pattern *"Jungfernsteig"* (maidens' path) of mellow earth tones, and below is "Palmyre" in cheerful, sunny shades.

A wonderful bracelet which combines faceted round and marquis stones of brown and iridescent coloring onto a linked chain backing. The spectacular earrings, featuring topaz cabochons with iridescent and pearl stones, were made by Schauer of Fifth Avenue, c. 1960.

These two pair of earclips by Beau feature topaz brown marquis stones with iridescent chatons in pretty, floral arrangements.

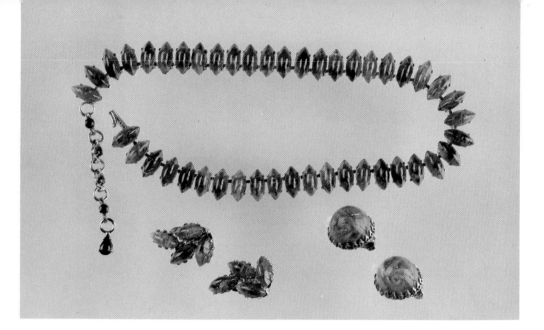

Mottled dark amber cabochons of round and marquis shape are used by Schreiner without further embellishment for the choker and earclips so that the beauty of the stones themselves can be seen.

Citrine yellow faceted beads with special iridescent short and long beads made a surprisingly delicate necklace by Alice Caviness with pendant balls of openwork and green rhinestones, c. 1960.

Opposite page:
Mottled amber rhinestones are caught in a net of grey and pearl stones for this smashing bib necklace by Schreiner, c. 1965.

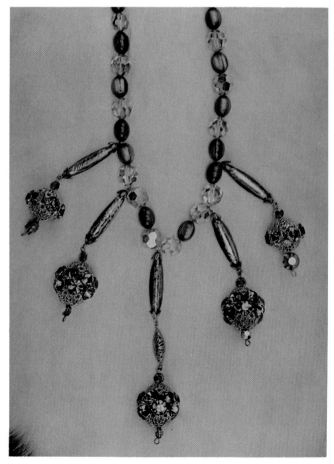

Pearl

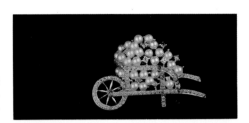

What a delight! The front wheel of this barrow brooch actually turns. The mound of glass pearls and clear chatons were a truly inspired design by Jomaz, c. 1960.

A most delicate lace design was made into this choker of glass pearls and clear rhinestones by Kramer of New York for Christian Dior, c. 1960. Cobra & Bellamy

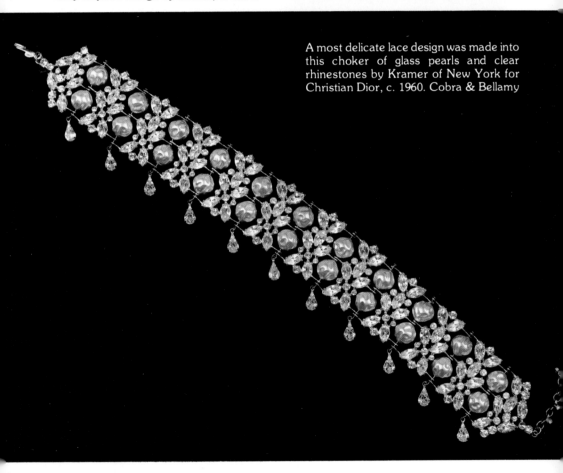

Opposite page:
Glass pearls of every shape, size and color have been used for jewelry for centuries. These examples from the mid-twentieth century demonstrate the fine crafts-manship which made costume jewelry so important in those years. The intricately woven lace bracelet shown at the bottom of the picture was designed by Mitchel Maer for Christian Dior in 1953. Fior

Exotic Baroque glass pearls are framed by a geometric design of baguette diamond rhinestones in this bold brooch and earclip set by Schreiner. The black pearls in the flowerhead earclips, also by Schreiner, are varied in size to give naturalistic variety to the otherwise regular arrangement.

Four strands of handmade Clio baroque glass pearls are joined by Austrian faceted crystal half-barrel emerald green rhinestones for this jeweled Bridge necklace and button earclips made by R. F. Clark, c. 1970 for Wm. de Lillo USA. Wm. de Lillo Archive

A sensational pearl fringe necklace hand-constructed with round and pear-shaped glass pearls and German crystal cabochon emerald green rhinestones. The necklace and matching button earclips were designed by R. F. Clark, c. 1970 for Wm. de Lillo USA. Wm. de Lillo Archive

Earclips of glass half pearls set in a gold bezel with geometric rhinestone embellishments made by Holly Hill.

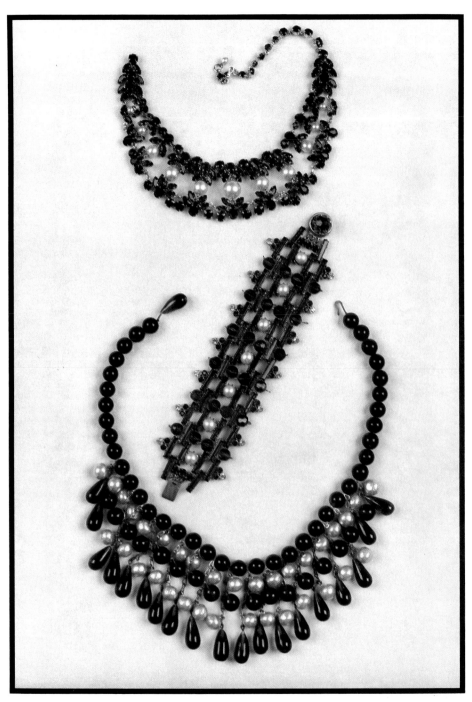

Pearls add the accents rather than the forms in these designs. The delicate choker necklace features ruby red faceted rhinestones in a floral garland design by Christian Dior, c. 1959. The bracelet and fringe necklace, however, use colored glass beads to carry out the bold designs of unknown makers from the 1940s. Fior

Seed pearls distinguish this important jeweled butterfly brooch with German glass cabochons of emerald, amethyst, ruby, pink, and hematite rhinestones and an acrylic pear-shaped, fluted clear center. The brooch was hand constructed with superimpositions and designed by R. F. Clark, c. 1969-70 for Wm. de Lillo USA. Wm. de Lillo Archive

The large pendant glass pearl is carried by a brooch full of light and fantasy due to its expanding design and unfoiled rhinestones of many colors and shapes and the glass pearl accents. The brooch and matching earclips were made by Schreiner, c. 1965.

Two hinged cuff bracelets by Wm. de Lillo and R. F. Clark for Wm. de Lillo USA are shown with ridged tubing, jewels and seed pearls, c. 1969. On the left, 18kt gold electroplated tubing is wired with seed pearls, Swarovski faux square diamonds and emeralds and glass pearl endings on each side. On the right, the silverplated tubing is wired with seed pearls and cut steel seeds and glass pearl endings are on each side. Wm. de Lillo Archive.

A string of pearls and so much more. This choker necklace by Coro is embellished with a flexible panel of floral design incorporating seed pearls and rhinestones.

Large baroque pearls of tear-drop shape are clustered with rhinestones in gold-colored settings to create a dramatic, though unmarked, brooch and matching pendant ear clips.

Masterfully designed in 1961, this glass pearl drop brooch by Christian Dior has a sophisticated, symmetrical pattern of elegant marquis rhinestones. The pearl and amethyst colored bead necklace, also by Christian Dior, supports a complex pendant cluster with three pearl drops. Cobra & Bellamy

Glass pearls on radiating tendrils expand the floral design of the colored rhinestones in the unmarked brooch.

Two unmarked brooches utilize the soft lustre of glass pearls to achieve their dynamic, artistic designs. At the top, large pearls contrast unbacked, faceted crystal rhinestones in a very pleasing triangular geometric pattern. Below, pearls dangle in a cluster like grapes below a gold mesh bow.

From two strands of irregular glass pearl beads, a lacy pearl and rhinestone fringe pendant is suspended in this classic design by Miriam Haskell.

143

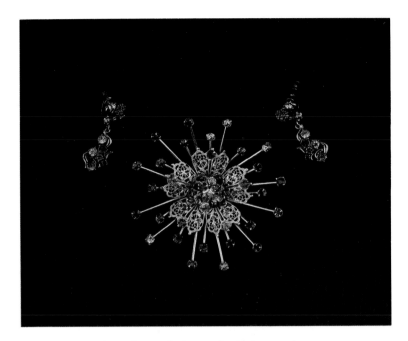

A starburst design and spectrum colors
are captured in this unmarked brooch and
the matching eardrops probably made in
Bohemia in the 1930s.

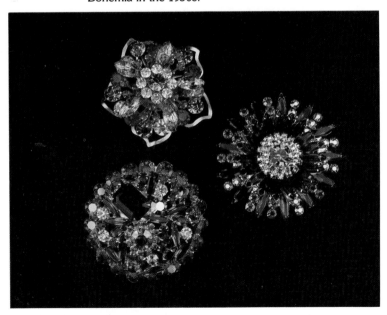

The iridescent stones pick up colored light
from the surrounding colored rhinestones
in these three unmarked brooches from
the 1960s.

4. Combined colors and stones

A ribbon of individual emerald cut and marquis rhinestones loops gracefully to form this unmarked bow brooch and the matching earclips, c. 1955.

Fine faceted, marquis, pastel rhinestones are framed with chatons and linked with glass pearls to create this smashing set by Schreiner.

Breathtaking! This truly exceptional matching set is copyrighted 1950 by Hollycraft. The delicate settings contain pastel rhinestones of varying sizes, a Hollycraft tradition, to produce an uncommonly pretty ensemble.

Compositions in blue and green had their time of popularity in the late 1960s. This group presents the color combination in beads, enamels and rhinestones on various forms of jewelry, but only the link bracelet is marked, and that is by Ciner.

Two pair of earrings and a bracelet, all marked "Art," combine colored rhinestones and gold settings in different styles, but the quality of each is consistently high.

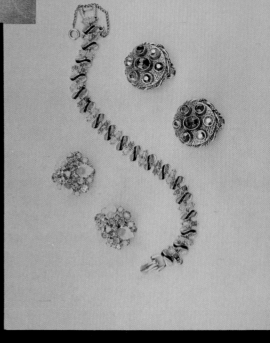

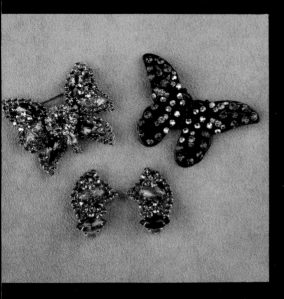

The elusive butterfly caught the imaginations of hundreds of jewelry designers in the 1960s because with this form imaginations could soar and utilize all combinations of rhinestone materials. The butterfly brooch with matching earclips includes several styles of special rhinestones and many colors; they are unsigned. The butterfly with black wire frame was made by Florenza.

147

Buckles and belts were a specialty of the Schreiner team who catered to the couture clientele. These accents for fine clothing utilize the highest quality materials in superb designs with top quality workmanship. Careful scrutiny of the rhinestones and settings of these belts by Schreiner is always a pleasurable use of your time. They all have a little bit of extra personality.

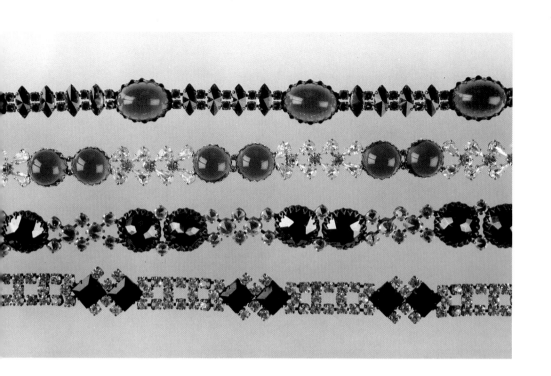

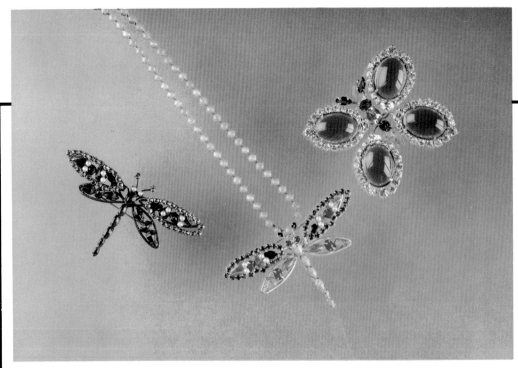

Fluttering dragonflies and butterflies in all the pastel shades were created by Schreiner in these brooches, necklace, belt and even a hair ornament. They are so much fun to see!

Sapphire blue, coral pink and turquoise German glass cabochons carefully bezel set are beautifully mounted in this gold electroplated brooch with flower motif figures and pedant earclips designed by R. F. Clark for Adolfo in 1969. Their sensitivity to the materials gives the jewelry a very special appearance.

The domed Maltese cross brooch and matching earrings were hand constructed with German crystal faux emerald, sapphire, ruby, and amethyst stones and Swarovski crystal pronged faux diamonds in rhodium plated settings. The design and creation were by R. F. Clark, c. 1970 for Wm. de Lillo USA. Wm. de Lillo Archive

This pair of button earrings by Eugene combines colored stones with gold beads and a deep frame for a tailored look rather unusual for rhinestones.

The two brooches to the left were made by Weiss in identical arrangements but with differently shaded colors, green and brown. The brooch to the right, in blue stones, is by Regency, yet how very similar the designs appear to be.

Here Weiss has combined cabochon and faceted stones of different colors with gold wire accents to create another round brooch and its matching earclips.

For these brooches by Weiss, rhinestones of different colors and textures, sizes and shapes are combined to create the designs. The yellow leaf and the red cluster, though, are entirely different in their finished appearance.

This is Kramer of New York's clustered brooch with diverse rhinestones tied right up with a gold mesh ribbon, a novel design!

Schreiner's Maltese cross brooch makes an interesting comparison with the de Lillo and Clark design shown above. The green and blue cabochon brooch, also by Schreiner, is kept from looking heavy, despite its large stones, because the design uses contrasting colors in an open arrangement.

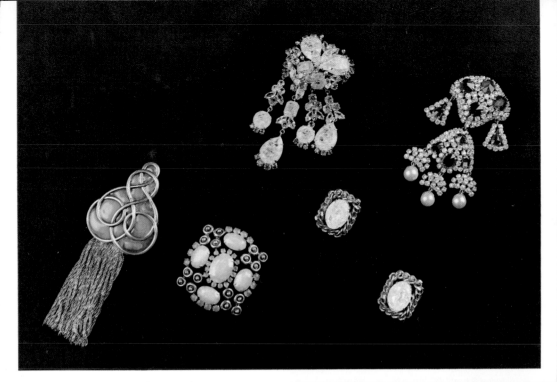

Grosse of Germany designed each of these brooches and earrings in 1969 for Christian Dior. Their diversity of materials is remarkable and demonstrates how fashions at the time embraced a broad range of styles, from glitter to metal chain.

Gold has always been an important look in costume jewelry, and here are examples embellished with different rhinestones. The turquoise and pearl studded "star" link bracelet was an inspired design by Marcel Boucher, one of the leaders in this broad field. The diamond studded bracelet and two brooches were made by Castlecliff.

Wide-ranging designs stylistically, all of this jewelry was made by Grosse of Germany for Christian Dior from 1962 to 1969, as follows: the large cross brooch in the center, 1962; the leaf brooch to the right with light green stones, 1963; the oval brooch with red center and the sapphire blue brooch with drop pearl, 1964; the bracelet, 1967; and the matching brooch and earclips, 1969. What an interesting decade for fashion. Fior

Leaf designs were common in costume jewelry, and here are some by the best designers, all with rhinestone embellishment. The two brooches at the left, with black enamel and the three-leaf design, are by Marcel Boucher. The intriguing openwork design is by Sandor. The leaf with green rhinestones is by Trifari.

In these necklaces, Schreiner combined mottled jade glass with pearls and dark sapphire blue faceted stones on the left, and clear green rocks with colored cabochons and pearls in the pendant on the right.

References

American Jewelry Manufacturing, May 1962, p.18-22.

Hoffer, Otto. "Glass stones, a fascinating industry," **American Jewelry Manufacturers**, March, 1972, p.18, 32, 33, 35, 36, 37.

Hoffer, Otto. **Imitation Gemstones**, Random Personal Reminiscences, 1980, privately printed.

Goetz, Marcia, trans., "The Life of Daniel Swarovski, Told by Himself," (from articles in *The Werkgeitung of Daniel Swarovski*, Wattens, Austria.)

Weisberg, Alfred M., "Why Providence?", 1988, Technic, Inc, Providence Jewelers Museum.

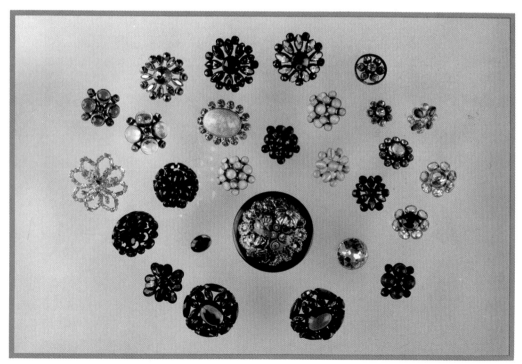

Buttons are an important part of the rhinestone world, too. These buttons by Schreiner from the 1950s added glamour to the clothing of their couture clients who included all the best-known names in American designs.

Price Guide

Values vary immensely according to an article's condition, location of the market, parts of the country, materials, craftsmanship, demand and overall quality of design. While one must make their own decisions, we can relate estimates from our survey of different markets to act merely as a guide. Values are in U. S. dollars.

p. 1.	set	2800-3300
p. 2.	pins	100-200
	bracelet	175-250
	drop pin	275-350
p. 3.	cuff	125-175
	pink links	150-225
	Am. green	175-225
	Gm. link	150-225
p. 4.	pendants	35-80
	earrings	45-60
p. 5.	set	200-325
p. 6.	sets	95-125
p. 7.	tulip pin	80-95
	filigree pin	65-95
p. 8.	bracelet	750-850
p. 10.	set	900-1100
p. 11.	bracelets	300-500each
p. 12.	set	1500-1700
p. 13.	earrings	65-95
	brooches	85-110
p. 14.	pearl necklace	200-300
	turq. set	150-200
p. 15.	pin	95-125
p. 16.	bracelets	95-150
p. 17.	brooches	125-175
p. 18.	pins	125-175
p. 19.	bracelet	85-120
	Regency pins	65-100
	earrings	75-110
	Schreiner brooches	125-175
p. 20.	pendants	125-165
p. 22.	pins	175-250
	set	150-200
p. 23.	purple pins	100-150
	Lee pins	65-95
	Lee earrings	60-90
p. 24.	top brooches	60-90
	Schreiner brooches	85-100
p. 25.	brooch	125-175
	necklace	75-100
p. 27.	brooches	175-250
	earclips	60-90
p. 28.	belt clasps	175-250
	earclips	150-200
p. 29.	set	1000-1500
p. 30.	Cross set	1400-1700
	Geometric Tie	1000-1300
p. 31.	set	750-950
p. 33.	necklaces	175-250
	group	95-125
p. 34.	necklace	475-600
	bracelet & earrings	300-375
p. 35.	necklace	500-600
p. 36.	set	375-450
	brooch	85-125
p. 37.	necklace set	3500-4200
	bracelet set	300-400
p. 39.	brooch	900-1200
	earrings	45-60
p. 40.	set	1500-1800
p. 41.	wreath brooch	125-175
	cross brooches	175-225
p. 43.	set	125-175
	earrings	75-100
	earrings	50-75
	pendant	95-135
p. 44.	top bracelet	175-250
	top brooches	95-125
	bottom bracelet	350-450
	bottom brooches	125-175
p. 45.	crystal group	150-200
	millifiori	175-250
	set	1200-1700
p. 47.	set	600-800
p. 48.	hair ornament	175-250
	garland	85-120
	cluster	95-125
p. 49.	brooch & earclips	65-90
	red brooch	65-95
	pink earrings	50-80
	wreath	75-100
	cluster brooch	50-65
	drop earrings	65-90
p. 50.	necklace set	250-300
	brooch set	125-180
p. 51.	group	500-700
p. 52.	pendant	95-125
	top brooches	50-70
	bottom brooch	60-90
	bracelets	125-170
p. 53.	bracelet	100-140
	brooches	90-125
	set	100-125
p. 54.	cuff	125-175
p. 55.	necklace	375-450
p. 56.	top necklace	150-195
	cuff bracelets	85-100
	black bracelet	95-120
	green necklace	75-100
p. 57.	top set	120-150
	earrings	50-70
	necklaces	75-100
p. 58.	choker & bracelet	800-1100
	set	350-500
	necklaces	350-450
	earrings	95-125
p. 59.	earrings	200-275
	pins	150-225
	choker	100-175
p. 60.	set	1200-1400
p. 61.	star brooches	175-250
p. 62.	crystal necklace	900-1400
	jewelled necklace	900-1400
p. 63.	brooch	150-225
	Pineapple necklace	1500-1900
	tiara	35-50
p. 64.	Jomaz brooches	100-150
	openwork brooch	125-175
	Trifari earrings	90-130
	Pell brooches	50-70
	Ciro brooch	75-100
	Polcini brooches	95-135
p. 65.	earrings	150-200
	brooches	450-600
	choker & earclips	250-300
p. 66.	hair ornaments	25-80
	necklace	300-400
	earclips	90-120
p. 67.	brooch & earclips	200-275
	Ciner bracelet	90-125
	earrings	65-90
	stone bracelet	75-100
	brooches	70-95
p. 68.	cross brooch	90-120
	girandole brooch	125-175
	Carnegie earclips	70-100
	huge earclips	65-90
	crescent earclips	120-150
p. 69.	Carnegie necklace	120-170
	Ciner bracelet	95-130
	Coro set	150-225
p. 70.	brooch	225-300
	halter	special
p. 71.	necklace	275-350
	leaf clips	175-250
	ear clips	75-100
	brooch	150-225
p. 72.	necklace	225-300
	earrings	65-100
	brooch	90-135
p. 73.	drop earrings	75-120
	parure	500-650
	choker & earrings	250-300
	necklace	175-225
	Vogue earrings	65-100
p. 74.	brooch	175-250
	set	225-300
p. 75.	necklace	375-475
	brooches	175-250
p. 76.	top set	125-200
	brooch	125-175
	bottom set	150-225
p. 77.	set	400-500
p. 78.	top set	900-1200
	bottom set	900-1200
p. 79.	top set	850-1200
	bracelet	800-1000
	earrings & bracelet	1000-1200
p. 80.	top set	300-350
	bottom set	350-425
p. 81.	Trifari set	225-275
	brooch	200-300
	set	325-400
p. 82.	necklace set	300-400
	brooch	75-100
p. 83.	bouquet brooch	60-85
	pin & earclips	125-175
	pendant earrings	150-200
	butterfly brooch	125-175
	floral brooch	100-130
p. 84.	trapezoids necklace	95-125
	round stones necklace	100-135
	brooch & earclips	85-100

	left bracelet	150-200
	bracelet & pin	175-225
p. 85.	necklace	1200-1500
	drop pendant	175-200
p. 86.	brooches	65-85
	earrings	60-90
	necklace	1200-1500
p. 87.	spoke pin	75-95
	brooches	95-125
	pendant	100-125
p. 88.	collar	1000-1200
	brooch	200-250
p. 89.	brooch	800-1000
	set	450-550
p. 90.	leaf brooch	175-225
	lyre earclips	35-50
	bracelet & ear pendants	100-125
	brooch & earclips	85-110
p. 91.	brooch & earclips	350-425
	Shah of Iran set	900-1100
p. 92.	articulated necklace	1700-2000
	brooch & earclips	1200-1400
	trapeze necklace	1200-1500
p. 93	set	1500-2000
p. 94.	Givenchy earclips	95-125
	pendant	150-185
	openwork earrings	65-90
	necklace	150-200
	bracelet	200-300
	brooch	750-900
p. 95.	set	75-95
	pendant	800-1000
	Carnegie bangle	90-120
	Lane bangle	100-130
	cabochon bangle	125-150
p. 96	Kashmir set	400-500
	pin & earrings	125-150
	bracelet & earrings	125-150
	cluster earrings	60-90
p. 97.	earrings	50-70
	floral brooch	60-90
	single clips	150-185
	double clip	200-245
p. 98.	set	400-500
p. 99.	bracelet & earclips	1300-1700
	brooch	150-200
	earrings	85-125
p. 100.	Weiss	75-110
	Schreiner pin	65-95
p. 101.	key ring	50-75
	set	125-175
p. 102.	necklace	125-180
	bracelet	85-125
	brooch	90-120
	brooch & earclips	175-225
p. 103.	necklace & earclips	200-250
p. 104.	necklace & earrings	95-135
	red brooches	45-80
	brooch	35-60
	cuff bracelets	85-120
p. 105.	apples set	75-110
	oranges set	45-60
	strawberries set	45-60
	Vendome set	200-275
p. 106.	brooches	175-225
	pendant	250-300
p. 107.	brooch & earclips	50-75

	large brooches	225-275
	bracelet	250-285
p. 108.	top group	95-120
	bottom set	100-140
p. 109.	top necklace	95-130
	Lane set	375-450
p. 110.	sunflower set	200-250
	dragonfly	200-250
	floral brooch	150-200
	black wires brooch	125-175
p. 111.	brooch & earrings	250-300
	brooch	150-200
p. 112.	set	450-600
p. 113.	brooch	170-200
	earclips & cuff	2000-2400
p. 114.	left earrings & bracelet	75-100
	right bracelet & earrings	85-110
p. 115.	pendant	85-130
	bracelet	65-90
	cross brooch	85-120
	flowerhead brooch	70-100
p. 116.	daisy brooch	75-100
	ivory brooch	85-110
	cornflower brooch	95-120
p. 117.	set	300-400
p. 118.	necklace & bracelet	1200-1500
	choker	75-100
	brooch & earclips	75-110
p. 119.	set	1200-1600
	scatter pins	75-100
p. 120	bib & earclips	800-1000
p. 121.	cluster brooch	50-95
	set	250-300
p. 122.	left set	200-250
	bracelet & earrings	200-250
	bracelet	95-120
p. 123.	brooch & earrings	275-375
	buckles	90-120
p. 124.	choker	1200-1600
	brooches	65-95
	pendant	50-75
p. 125.	brooch & earrings	160-200
	necklace & earclips	1200-1500
p. 126.	set	300-375
p. 127.	top set	1200-1600
	cuff bracelet	600-800
	necklace & earrings	800-1000
	bowtie clip	600-900
	small bowtie brooch	250-400
p. 128.	top set	1000-1200
	bottom set	800-1000
p. 129.	necklace	600-800
p. 130.	Pineapple Pin	50-65
	topaz earclips	45-7
	brooch & earclips	85-110
p. 131.	Austria brooch	45-70
	earclips	30-45
	set	250-300
p. 132.	brooch & earclips	250-350
	necklaces	175-225
p. 133.	bracelet	70-95
	Schauer earrings	60-90
	Beau earrings	65-95
p. 134.	bib necklace	300-400
p. 135.	choker & earclips	200-245
	necklace	200-275
p. 136.	bracelet	275-325

p. 137.	brooch	225-295
	choker	300-400
p. 138.	brooch & earclips	300-400
	flowerhead earclips	100-150
	necklace & earclips	2500-3000
p. 139.	necklace & earclips	2600-3000
	H. Hill earclips	65-90
p. 140.	Dior necklace	350-400
	bracelet	250-300
	fringe necklace	275-350
p. 141.	butterfly brooch	2000-2400
	brooch & earclips	350-450
	cuff bracelets	900-1200
p. 142.	choker	295-375
	brooch & earclips	200-275
	Dior drop brooch	300-400
	Dior necklace	400-500
p. 143.	floral brooch	120-150
	triangular brooch	150-180
	grapes & bow brooch	175-225
	necklace	450-600
p. 144.	brooch & eardrops	90-120
	bottom brooches	200-275
p. 145.	brooch & earclips	100-130
	set	800-1000
p. 146.	earrings	65-95
	bracelet	125-150
	set	450-550
p. 147.	necklace	120-150
	bracelet	100-140
	earrings	50-70
	brooch	75-100
	brooch & earclips	100-140
	black butterfly	75-95
p. 148-		
149.	belts	95-325
p. 150.	brooches	125-200
	necklace	150-200
	belt	150-225
	hair ornament	75-95
p. 151.	brooch & earclips	800-1100
	cross brooch & earrings	1200-1400
p. 152.	top left brooches	75-110
	top right brooches	95-150
	brooch & earclips	110-150
p. 153.	earrings	65-95
	Kramer brooch	130-160
	cross brooch	285-350
	cabochon brooch	200-275
p. 154.	top brooches	300-400
	earrings	75-110
	Boucher bracelet	350-500
	Castlecliff bracelet	120-150
	Castlecliff brooches	70-100
p. 155.	brooches	250-350
	bracelet	300-400
	earclips	70-100
p. 156.	black brooch	150-200
	leaf brooch	170-220
	openwork brooch	150-200
	green brooch	125-200
	necklace	250-300
	pendant	275-350
p. 157.	buttons	50-100

Index

Adolfo 56, 151
Arden, Elizabeth 22
Art 147
Attwood and Sawyer 71
Aurora Borealis 47, 48, 49
beads 55
Beau 133
Bogoff 67, 85
Boucher 28, 70, 154, 156
cabochons 27
Carnegie, Hattie 68, 69, 89, 95
Carven 71, 86
Castlecliff 154
Caviness, Alice 135
Chanel, Coco 16
chatons 21
Ciner 67, 69, 94, 147
Clark, Robert F. 10, 11, 12, 30, 37, 39, 40, 45, 58, 62, 63, 78, 85, 86, 89, 91, 92, 94, 99, 113, 118, 119, 124, 125, 127, 128, 138, 139, 140, 151
Clio pearls 138
Coppola & Toppo 54, 58
Coro 69, 71, 97, 109, 142
Cortez, Hernando 7
Coventry, Sarah 15, 114
crystal 62
cubic zirconia 62
de Lillo, William 10, 11, 12, 30, 37, 39, 40, 45, 58, 62, 63, 78, 85, 86, 89, 91, 94, 99, 113, 118, 119, 124, 125, 127, 128, 138, 139, 140, 151
Dior, Christian 14, 43, 117, 132, 137, 140, 142, 155
Doddz 49

doublets 23
drop shape 33
Eisenberg 64, 123
Eisenhower, Mamie 22
Eugene 152
Florenza 43, 50, 14
Gablonz 7, 9, 11, 13, 14, 47, 96
Givenchy 94
Gonthiez Freres 71
Grosse of Germany 43, 122, 132, 154, 155
Haskell, Miriam 143
hematite 47
Holly Hill 139
Hollycraft 76, 146
Jomaz 64, 71, 137
Joseff of Hollywood 29
Kandell and Marcus, New York 36
Kaufbeuren 15
Keyes 48
Kramer of New York 84, 104, 137, 153
Lane, Kenneth Jay 95, 109
Lee, Judith 23
LeSage 37, 58
Linz 15
Lisner 39, 118
Maer, Mitchel 14, 137
Mazer, Joseph 33, 56
Napier 77
Neugablonz 15, 16, 17, 47, 77, 117
Norell, Norman 16
Pell 64
pendants 33
Polcini 64
Polo, Marco 7
Regency 19, 52, 152

Ricci, Nina 3
Riedel, Josef 13, 47
Sandor 156
sapphire 62, 77
scalloped stones 39
Schauer of Fifth Avenue 133
Schiaparelli, Elsa 16, 64, 65, 132
Schreiner 16, 17, 18, 19, 21, 22, 24, 27, 28, 33, 34, 35, 36, 41, 45, 48, 50, 51, 60, 63, 67, 70, 73, 74, 76, 79, 80, 81, 83, 85, 86, 88, 90, 91, 94, 98, 99, 100, 101, 102, 103, 107, 110, 111, 115, 119, 120, 129, 130, 135, 138, 140, 145, 148, 150, 153, 157
Schwabish Gemuend 15
Sherman 25
spinel 62
Swarovski, Daniel, & Co. 8, 9, 10, 12, 13, 86, 92, 99, 113, 127, 140
Swoboda of California 31
Triad 43
Trifari 45, 64, 81, 82, 102, 156
Turnau 7
Vendome 53, 58, 105, 125
Vogue 49, 73
Warner 48, 49
Wattens 10, 11, 12
Weis, Eduard and Company 8, 9
Weiss 52, 81, 100, 105, 118, 152, 153
Ytrium-aluminum-garnet (yag) 62